THE
SPOUSE
GAP

THE
SPOUSE
GAP

Weathering the Marriage Crisis During Middlescence

Robert Lee &
Marjorie Casebier

ABINGDON PRESS—NASHVILLE—NEW YORK

THE SPOUSE GAP

ISBN 0-687-39258-6

Library of Congress Catalog Card Number: 75-160795

SET UP, PRINTED, AND BOUND BY THE
PARTHENON PRESS, AT NASHVILLE,
TENNESSEE, UNITED STATES OF AMERICA

PREFACE

Have you wondered why so many couples, married for a dozen or fifteen years, suddenly find it difficult to keep their marriage boat from rocking? Compatibility in early marriage is no guarantee against the spouse gap—the drifting, growing apart, or divergence in interest and behavior so as to be quite ill mated by the time middle age arrives.

This book is about the impact of the "middlescent" years on marriage. Behind the contrived facade of many marriages lurks a deadly disease—the middlescent malaise. For those afflicted by this disease the life and spice may expire from their marriage and the emptiness of their relationship become exposed.

Our intent is to stimulate recognition and reflection, to shed light on a pervasive problem that affects many, if not all, married couples. No easy answers are suggested, although some guidelines and pointers for bridging the spouse gap are presented in the final chapter.

A panel of fifty couples was interviewed to provide personal data and case material for the study. In the text we will have frequent occasion to refer to this information as derived from our "Marriage Interview Schedule." Yet it should be clear that we are not seeking to report a "scientific" study. This book is written in nontechnical language for the nonspecialist reader. Hopefully, it is self-help literature in the best understanding of that term. It is addressed to spouses who value their marriage and genuinely wish to improve the quality of married life.

Alas, analysis has a way of clarifying and, at the same time, distorting reality. We may become so preoccupied with problems that we would have to express sheer amazement that the institution of marriage still stands—much like the happily married couple who read a book about family conflict and became so disturbed by the difficulties that they wondered why they ever got married in the first place!

The authors are concerned with *honesty* in marital relations—not in the lip-service manner of "motherhood" or "apple pie," but in the ofttimes painful sense of "facing marriage like it was," "telling it like it is," and "imagining it like it might be."

Finally, we wish to express our indebtedness to many sources, both written and oral: our panel of informants, business and professional groups who have heard and responded to the material in lecture form, our battery of diligent typists, Thelma Furste, Ruby Egnew, and Gertrude Shaul. Our appreciation, in full measure, goes also to May and the five little Lees, Mellanie, Marcus, Matthew, Wendy, and Michele, for spouse and family support, to Elizabeth and Gene for friendly encouragement, and to a host of friends who may imagine that they are reading the story of their lives in these pages.

RL and MC

CONTENTS

PROLOGUE: SPOUSE AND SPICE IN DRAMATIC PERSPECTIVE

Almost everyweek we hear that some couple we know is in serious trouble or about to split up after establishing what on the surface seems to be an idyllic marriage. Such consistent experience may lead us to observe that while the plural of *mouse* is always *mice,* only rarely does it seem accurate to describe the plural of *spouse* as *spice!* Indeed, we have a spouse gap because marriage has lost its spice. Two people who have been propelled into marriage by an intense and passionate desire to be together forever often find that the exciting flavor of their relationship has not lasted.

Such loss of the essential ingredients which give spice to the marriage relationship does not happen overnight. It usually turns out to be the end result of a gradual process, a kind of erosion of the taste buds until general blandness characterizes the marital diet. And, being the kind of creature he is, man does not finally settle comfortably into a bland state of being. Sooner or later a memory is reawakened, or a passion rekindled, or a longing reborn, and then he (or she) becomes frustrated and dissatisfied. The desire for some spice in life reasserts itself with insistence, and the familiar old spouse scarcely seems like the person with whom to find it.

In previous decades it was commonly supposed that if two people could survive the first *five* years of life together they could look forward to making it through the rest of their married lives with relatively little difficulty. And if the marriage did not stay forever as exciting as anticipated, it had sufficient foundation to provide for the cultivation of similar basic tastes concerning family, home, and security. Now, however, those problems which shake a marriage during its first five years seem only to submerge in the life of the couple as they deal with the immediate pressures of day-to-day problems and then resurface ten or twenty years later when their situation appears to be relatively calm and free from financial worries.

Why does marriage summon us to life fulfillment only to turn into an empty dream or a living hell for many people? How does love get lost in marriage, and can it ever be rediscovered by the same two people together? Why do two people freely enter the bond of marriage with high hopes and then experience the bond as a chain preventing them from finding the "real" relationship they've always longed for, or from at least enjoying a "last fling" before senescence sets in?

This kind of gathering distance and growing apart of two people in marriage is another facet of the general "gaposis" which afflicts our society as its struggles with changing role expectations and value systems. We are, of course, familiar with the generation gap. Young people say "You can't trust anyone over thirty," and youth and adults seem to look at each other from different worlds. We have that glaring gap between the rich nations and the poor nations, between the haves and the have-nots. Then there is the credibility gap. Our nation, in short, is shot through with gaps of alienation —between the young and the old, the rich and the poor, the white and the black, the talkers and the doers. To our lexicon of gaps, therefore, it is appropriate to add the notion of the "spouse gap," which comes very close to the experience of every married person at one time or another, and which aptly depicts the situation leading to the disenchantment or the disengagment of marriage partners after ten or twenty years together. It is said that one-third of all marriages now end in divorce within ten years, while no one knows how many of the remaining two-thirds are precarious, or how many of them might be called "emotional divorces." No one knows how many couples live together in broken homes.

Many cultural changes contribute to the spouse gap problem. New and reliable forms of birth control are leading to different views of sexual morality before and during marriage. Better health and increased longevity mean that two people who marry in their twenties can look forward to as many or more years together without children in the home as they have with them. The shift in the importance of work in human life, from being the central preoccupation, leaves couples having to deal with their relationships in terms of more leisure time together. Ever increasing mobility continues to scatter families, causing loneliness, uprootedness, uneasiness in making neighborhood friends, and uncertain futures. Divorce no longer carries with it the social stigma it once did, and new divorce laws will make it easier for couples to part amicably. Greater independence for women means that they are not as dependent on marriage as they once were for status and security. The emergence of the Women's Liberation Movement is a sign that women have had their noses pressed against the window pane for too long and will no longer tolerate being left outside in the cold.

Marriage is extremely sensitive to the galloping cultural changes of our day. Such cultural changes leave us facing a number of paradoxes as we wrestle with the transition from a traditional concept of marriage to some new understanding: there are more marriages now *and* more divorces; greater financial resources for families *and* greater debts; more independence and freedom for both sexes *and* greater insecurity about establishing and maintaining personal relationships. Surely another paradox is that even so-called good marriages are vulnerable to the spouse gap. Given the rising level of expectations nowadays, it is not just the worst marriages that are in trouble, but also the best ones. It may be high-order discontent when good marriages are suddenly aware that they might become better, but it is like the paradox on campus, where the best, most prestigious universities in the nation are in turmoil, not the worst ones.

Nowhere is the marriage revolution taking a greater toll than within the ranks of the middle-aged. For one thing, the members of this group have been the victims of almost constant social upheaval. Born during or not long after World War I, they suffered the impact of the Depression, were just in time to bear the brunt of the fighting in World War II, then had to adjust to increasing urbanization and technology, and now are facing the disintegration of the very institutional value systems on which they have built their lives. Secondly, the present middle-agers entered the married state with many romantic illusions about what that relationship would mean. "Boy meets girl, boy loses girl, boy gets girl, and boy and girl live happily ever after" was the great American Dream every person believed he could achieve. Finally, the period of middle age itself presents a unique and unforeseeable crisis in the life of each person. It is the time of agonizing reappraisal and self-questioning: Did I make the right decisions? Where do I go from here? Is this all there will be for me in life? These questions are, in turn, intensified for women by the physical changes brought about in menopause, and for men by the psychological-emotional fear of failure and the fear of losing sexual potency. On top of everything else, middlescents are the chief targets of attack by a militant youth generation which depicts middle-agers as square defenders of the establishment.

We are discovering middlescence to be a new stage in life that has long gone unrecognized. Our society pays so much attention to adolescence that we forget about middlescence. We are a kid-centered, kid-dominated culture. How ridiculous to see a sixty-year-old, mini-skirted grandmother seeking to ape teen-age life-styles. People over thirty-five and under fifty-five are a much neglected age group who are required to bear society's greatest burden of responsibility while being its most taken-for-granted group. The middle-aged adult trying to face his difficulties and solve his problems can take refuge neither in the inexperience of adolescence nor in the frailty of senescence. While we are familiar with race and class segregation, we have too often passed over this less familiar but more insidious factor of age segregation and prejudice. And while we have devoted much attention and study to the problems of the morning and evening of life, we have passed over the afternoon portion with the erroneous assumption that it did not need any special consideration. Yet one-fourth the population is in this age bracket.

It is now apparent that the pressures of middlescence itself have far-reaching implications for marriage and family life. Considering all these factors it probably comes as no surprise to us to learn that about 25 percent of divorces these days occur between people who have been married fifteen years or longer, and that figure seems to be growing. It is sad that so many marital relationships go awry just at the time in life when two people need each other perhaps the most.

While this situation is indeed understandable, it is the belief of the authors that it is not necessarily inevitable. If two people who have lived together as man and wife can come to terms with the reasons for the gap between them and can make an effort to close it, it is possible for them to enter a new phase in their life together with rewards far beyond their greatest expectations. For, while the spouse-gap crisis must be recognized as a cultural phenomenon, it can be dealt with at its most basic and personal point—the relationship between a particular husband and wife.

On its most practical level the spouse gap has to do simply with the broken or the closed channels of communication between husbands and wives, between two people who are in close physical proximity, but who may be drifting and experiencing a psychological distance in their relationship. T. S. Eliot captured this situation in *The Cocktail Party.*

One of his characters described the lives of a married couple as

> Two people who know they do not understand each other,
> Breeding children whom they do not understand
> And who will never understand them.[1]

In addition to the cultural changes that are affecting the traditional concept of marriage and the crisis inherent in the period of middlescence, we can then point ultimately to a basic lack of communication as the key to the spouse gap problem. Two people enter marriage on similar tracks, and if they do not make the effort to express their feelings and thoughts to each other they will sooner or later find themselves on parallel tracks and then at a divided fork in the road which represents a turning point. One of the characters in Lillian Hellman's play *Toys in the Attic*, faced with the truth of another person, makes a painful observation which expresses the situation for many couples: "Well, people change and forget to tell each other. Too bad—causes so many mistakes."

The spouse gap widens, certainly, wherever there is neglect, or when one partner grows and the other stands still, or when the focal point of the relationship remains fixed on past goals and dreams rather than on moving to new common pursuits and joint ventures. A primary characteristic of the spouse gap is its ability to occur and to grow almost unnoticed. On the surface the marriage may seem stable, secure, compatible. The couple, over the years, have established a comfortable pattern for their lives which is satisfying in many ways. But this very pattern, above all else, should be a warning sign. We must take seriously the great insight by Balzac: "Marriage must constantly conquer the monster that devours. The name of that monster is habit." Habits, patterns, routines,

---

[1] From T. S. Eliot, *Complete Poems and Plays* (New York: Harcourt, Brace and Co., 1952), p. 364. Used by permission of Harcourt Brace Jovanovich and Faber & Faber.

when they remain unexamined, lead finally to monumental boredom and ennui. The stable, dependable, orderly routine which once implied security in the marital relationship now becomes a drag, a marriage rut. Spouse ceases to imply spice in the marriage relationship, and the gap becomes an ugly ditch that divides and separates husband and wife.

The causes behind the breakdown in communication within marriage and the impact of middle-age on the marriage partners will be explored in considerably more detail in this book. Out of that understanding, then, attention will be focused on ways in which the spouse gap can become an opportunity for a renewed, integrated marriage, a deepening of life's most intimate relationship. Such a closing of the spouse gap starts with the necessity of really seeing the partner as a person, where he is now, then moves through hammering out certain practical things that will build a new way of life together, and goes on to look at the future possibilities for such a re-created marriage.

The overall organization for this volume has fallen quite naturally into a dramatic form that reflects an essential rhythm in human life. This rhythm, richly delineated and explored for us by the Greek dramatist Sophocles, basically involves the movement of the human spirit through the modes of purpose, passion, and perception. Or, said another way, as a man grows and develops through time and space he may directly experience his own inner, changing world in terms of a rhythm that begins with an active intention, moves to suffering caused by obstacles blocking achievement of that intention, and then progresses to new insight into experience that comes through the suffering. In Sophocles' play *Oedipus Rex* this rhythm provided both the overall structure for the drama and the form for each of the internal episodes.

In more recent times this realization of life's rhythm in dramatic terms was picked up and refined into a form known as the "well-made play." In perceiving that the well-made play has structural elements in common with the well-made marriage, we have been able to make use of certain playwriting terminology that is very helpful to our analysis on the spouse gap phenomenon: situation, conflcit, complication, suspense, crisis, climax, and resolution.

Such interaction between drama and marriage actually seems very appropriate, for certainly there is a sense in which the development of a marriage can be viewed as a dramatic paradigm for life itself. All relationships involve the process of communication and all are subject to the gaps that occur when the lines of communication are blocked. By focusing on the most intense, intimate, and constant kind of personal relationship of all, that between two people in marriage, it is possible for us to gain insight into the other areas of human interaction in the journey of life.

I

SITUATION: THE MARRIAGE MYSTIQUE

Of the making of jokes about marriage there is no end. For instance, there is the old saw which goes: "Marriage is love, love is blind; therefore, marriage is an institution for the blind." Or there is the quip that "all men are born free, but some get married."

Laugh at marriage though we may, the truth of the matter is that the vast majority aspire to the marital status. Indeed, most single young adults search intensely and sometimes desperately, with computer aid, to find a partner to join in the dance of married life. The so-called eligible bachelor is just that, eligible for marriage.

Thus the mating game—that discovery, pursuit, and capture of the right person with whom one is "to live happily ever after"—continues to pervade our conversations, popular songs, books, magazines, and movies. Even when the beaches are littered with the wrecks of broken marriages—family members, friends, the individual's own previous one (or more) —the single person still assumes he can and must find that single other person with whom he can enter the state of wedded bliss.

Although critics report its "incipient extinction," the persistent rumor that marriage is dead is indeed premature. A recent, best-selling study of extramarital love in contemporary America concludes with the observation that "the content and style of marriage are changing, but marriage itself is more popular than in the past; even the high divorce rate, still growing toward an unknown limit, is no sign of disaffection with marriage but only with unsatisfying marriage, for nearly six-sevenths of the divorced remarry." [1]

In this stage-setting chapter we seek to explore some traditional views of marriage and thereby unearth some seeds of the spouse gap that are inherent within the popular conception of marriage itself. Thus we will discuss: Falling in Love, The Courting Game, and Marriage Expectations—for Better or Worse.

There is, it would seem, a kind of mystique about marriage, a mysterious, paradoxical, and elusive quality of life uniquely present in the husband/wife relationship where ideally and inexplicably the whole becomes more than the sum of its parts. As with every good mystique, everyone pretends to understand it, to unravel this heart of mystery, but no one really does. Nor do we possess a special key to unlock the enigma; but we seek to cast light on the problem, to illuminate various dimensions of the unfathomable marriage mystique.

The impulse behind the marriage mystique can best be described in terms of the search for wholeness. While we are not arguing that it is necessary for a person to marry in order to be whole, we are saying that a special kind of wholeness is consummated in a good marriage. Experiencing our own unique "aloneness"—our flights from aloneness to nothingness—we yearn for relationships greater than ourselves. For the vast majority of people a primary relationship of intimacy is established with a person of the opposite sex, since wholeness involves a uniting, or "wedding," of the masculine and the feminine natures.

The marriage mystique is a discernible force drawing two people together, but in and of itself this mystique provides no assurance that the couple so attracted will make a satisfactory match. Once the myths about marriage are tested,

[1] Morton Hunt, *The Affair* (New York: World Publishing Co., 1969), p. 288.

many other forces come into play and have far-reaching implications.

In studying the discrepancy between expectation and realization in the lives of married couples now in the throes of middlescence, we have discovered three primary fields in the couple's prenuptial relationship where the seeds of future difficulty may have been planted: What was meant by "falling in love," how the courtship game was conducted, and the various expectations and images brought to the marriage itself. As these three subjects are briefly explored, the reader is asked to play a game of "remembering it like it was"—applying any descriptions and discoveries to his own experience. By looking backward squarely at the relationship with the marriage partner and "remembering it like it was," we will be enabled to now "face it like it is" and after that to "imagine what it can yet be."

FALLING IN LOVE

Ask any couple why they joined in matrimony and the overwhelming response is, "We fell in love." It may surprise some to learn that "falling in love"—so esteemed as the prerequisite for marriage today—was probably unknown in earlier periods of man's history. In tracing the origins of marriage and the family, Lederer and Jackson point out that "in primitive vocabularies there was no word for 'love.' "[2] Mating first occurred at random, an advantage under those conditions where life expectancy was under thirty years (and presumably everyone could be trusted) and where the larger the "gene pool," the better the chance for offspring to acquire adaptive potentialities. Gradually the women began to gather in groups, sharing the care of the children and giving mutual aid and encouragement, and to these groups the men would return from their hunting and fighting trips. Then with

[2] William J. Lederer and Don D. Jackson, M.D., *The Mirages of Marriage* (New York: W. W. Norton and Co., 1968), p. 27.

19

control over fire came the development of camps, and with the evolution of speech the groups could identify their own kind. Finally, with recognition of the incest taboo a kind of clan system came into being.

The important thing to note in this thumbnail sketch of the evolution of the family is the fact that in those early days the family existed primarily as a unit for physical survival, with everyone having to work long and hard for that purpose.

Thus the growth of civilization itself rests on the emergence of the family unit as the primary social group in human life, with marriage being the name for the contractual arrangement made by those starting a new family unit. From its inception as a means for *physical* survival, marriage as an institution subsequently became the primary unit for *economic* survival. And around each of these functions arose attendant structures and rules to meet the given situations. Today, however, the primary need that marriage serves is for *community,* for *psychological* and *emotional* survival and support.

This shifting emphasis to psychological and emotional support means, of course, a much greater emphasis on the interpersonal relationship of the marriage partners and on their initial attraction to each other. No longer is primary consideration given to whether a certain person would make a strong partner in the fight to survive physically or economically; the basic criterion for marriage is whether he or she evokes in me a certain vague feeling called "love." Mysteriously, I am supposed to know *it* or feel *it* when *it* hits me like a thunderbolt of lightning—POW! I'm in love with a wonderful girl! The question of the day is the one asked in the popular song of another generation: "What is this thing called love?"

Most of us will readily admit that our culture is preoccupied with the idea of romantic love, and, if we are honest, we must admit that we too are captive to its strong appeal.

Advertisers know this, of course, and capitalize on romance and sex to sell everything from cars to cigarettes to shampoo to aspirin. In romantic love the couple is always young and beautiful, carefree and happy when alone together, with no worries, no responsibilities, and an unending desire and capacity for making love. What a make-believe world! Romantic love as the sole basis for marriage is at best an illusion and at worst an impossibility. It is building a house of marriage on shifting sand. Inevitably flames flicker and ardors cool in the face of the mundane problems that confront every marriage and constantly challenge the relationship based on romance to become reconstituted.

In answer to the question on our Marriage Interview Schedule, "What did you expect your marriage to be like?" some responded "peaches and cream," "an unending honeymoon," "eternally romantic," "a Doris Day movie." Then, after sober reflection, all respondents went on to observe that they now know such naïve expectations were impossible to fulfill.

Yet something in all of us seems to continue to yearn for romantic love, for visions of Camelot, leaving us disappointed and disenchanted when the dream fades. Where did such a notion ever come from in the first place?

Denis de Rougemont's seminal work *Love in the Western World* traces the birth of romantic love to twelfth-century France, to embodiment in the myth of Tristan and Iseult, and to active expression in such forms as courtly love and chivalry. This tradition wherein the knight in shining armor faces danger for the reward of a smile or a scarf from his lady (whom he loves passionately but never possesses) has been perpetuated for us in the "western movie" and very recently in the television weekly "Then Came Bronson." Given the escalation of power in our day, Bronson rode a motorcycle instead of a horse; but in fine old tradition he rescued the girl but never married her. Such a romantic figure may enrich our lives by adding a tantalizing spice to our imaginations, but it plays havoc with our emotions when we confuse it with married love.

The reason the cult of romantic love continues to give us so much trouble is because the essential ingredient is a dark and compelling passion that drives a person to seek for the kind of ultimate and tragic union with his beloved which is finally possible only in death. In this sense, passion is bound up inextricably with suffering, and its flame is fed by the presence of obstacles that keep the lovers apart. Indeed, if all barriers should be overcome, the passion would die and disillusionment set in, since by definition the passionate desire is present in searching for infinite, ecstatic bliss and not in attaining it.

In its time the myth of Tristan actually proved to be a stabilizing force against the early breakdown of marriage. The story provided a framework within which the secret-passion element could find satisfaction in symbolic expression. Tristan and Iseult were romantic symbols who, caught up by forces of passion over which they seemed to have no control, were compelled to seek the consummation of a love that ultimately destroyed them. They were, de Rougemont concludes, not really in love with each other at all, but each was in love with love and with himself as the person in whom the erotic, blinding, all-absorbing passions surged. The myth offered an unconscious opportunity for vicarious relief of the savage, passionate love which the people instinctively knew could destroy them if they lived it out.

De Rougemont observes that this dangerous passion-element still pulses today beneath the skin of a society liberated from rigid morality. But what we do not understand about romantic passion-love is that it feeds on inherent obstacles and difficulties which cannot help bringing unhappiness, suffering, or even death if pursued with serious intensity. At present we find ourselves actually in the backwashes of the cult of romanticism which may take either of two different directions: (1) we may try to reconcile passion and marriage, become disillusioned, get divorced, and marry again, only to be disillusioned again (the vicious circle can go on indefinitely, as we know, from the records set by the celebrity jet set in our society, who can afford such conspicuous consumption) ; (2) or we may recognize that passion and marriage are irreconcilable and seek fulfillment of our passionate desires in extramarital affairs in which elements of the forbidden and the secretive provide fuel for the flame. This is where it's at for those who claim that "marriage kills love" and a "little on the side keeps love alive."

For the most part, however, we in America have created a bastardized version of romantic passion-love by trying to unite marriage with romantic love in the ingenuous assurance that this is possible. Since the 1920's, when the happy ending had its heyday, Americans have naïvely believed that love, true love, could overcome all obstacles and opposition. De Rougemont describes with obvious delight a story about a telephone strike in New York. The women operators received a call from a couple who wanted to get married and were trying to locate a justice of the peace. The operators decided that their situation was indeed an emergency and acted in their behalf, thereby revealing a natural belief of Americans that "when one loves one must get married instantly." [3]

Is there an alternative to romantic love? In raising this question we are racing ahead of ourselves and anticipating a discussion to be resumed in the final chapter.

THE COURTING GAME

A second area to discuss in the middlescent marriage game of remembering it like it was brings us back to our courting days. Intimations of the coming spouse gap often pop up while we are playing the courting game. Being aware of how

---

[3] Denis de Rougemont, *Love in the Western World*, tr. Montgomery Belgion (New York: Doubleday Anchor Books, 1956) , p. 304.

and why you got involved with your marriage partner may provide some clues on the nature of the gap which subsequently developed.

Meeting the right person with whom to enter the bond of wedlock is certainly no easy matter. One recognizes the truism behind the comedian's quip, "My father got to marry my mother, but I've got to go out and marry a perfect stranger!" Most of us follow a pattern of random dating in which we gradually build up knowledge of the opposite sex and of ourselves in that relationship. Then a particular person emerges from among the dating partners as more interesting or attractive or attentive than the others (and who experiences me the same way) and we advance to "going steady." This "going steady" may happen only once or it may happen a number of times, but at some point we then move on to becoming engaged and to marrying.

While we are accustomed to "dating-mating-and-debating," this American system has often been considered shocking in other cultures, though it is now practiced rather widely all over the world. A basic factor in the dating system is the freedom of two people to decide to relate to each other. Perhaps one thing we have not always admitted, however, is that this freedom operates within definite limits. For one thing, research has revealed that the greatest determiner in mate selection is sheer propinquity, which is to say, where you happen to live determines whom you meet.

But it is also true that this "freedom" by which we choose a person to date and, eventually, to marry is usually heavily cloaked in the kind of romantic aura we discussed previously. These emotional feelings are interpreted as love, but it is more likely that they are strong feelings of sexual desire, or fear of loneliness, or hunger for approval. People in love have often described the emotion they feel as ecstasy—which actually means a state of being in which the person is beside himself and beyond all reason and self-control. Hence they claim to be "madly in love." Such absorbing and overwhelming feelings of madness can hardly be deemed a proper state from which responsible freedom can be exercised!

With this general situation in mind let us look at some particular aspects of the "courtship routine" where difficulties may occur.

In the first place, all the players in the courting game are guilty of a good deal of dishonesty and deception. "From the simple best-foot-forward pretense to the all's-fair-in-love-and-war attitude, young people engage in a wide variety of shams and deceits which, when successful, often turn the 'victory' into a bitter disillusionment when the masks come off." [4] Too often the masks are retained well into marriage, but eventually are stripped, and the exposure is shocking. This masquerade is conducted largely out of fear that another person cannot love us as we really are, so we must try to make ourselves into what we think the other person will love. Since the other person may be doing the same thing, the ground is very shaky indeed. The courting game may well involve three selves, the real self being quite hidden. First, there is "Who John Really Is," or John I. Second, there is "Who John Projects Himself to Be," or John II. Finally, there is the "Person Mary Really Wants to See," or John III. The same applies to Mary. Here, then, are six people in search of two selves. Under the rules of the game it takes a long time for the "real" John and Mary to meet. Sooner or later in marriage, however, the real self will surface, and the partners will have to live with the genuine article.

The traditional role of women contributes also to the dishonesty and falseness fostered during courtship. Under the assumption of male superiority, woman has been driven to attract man by exploiting her physical points and by focusing attention on the man's needs and desires in a way that makes her own needs secondary. Such a lack of understand-

[4] Robert B. McLaren and Homer D. McLaren, *All to the Good: A Guide to Christian Ethics* (New York: World Publishing Co., 1969), pp. 75-76.

ing of the complementary function of the masculine and feminine in human sexuality has led to much frustration and disillusionment. The illusion that man can be fully human without woman is still a powerful belief, even though we suppose our age to be liberated from the old patriarchial hierarchy. In the business and professional world we see the assumption of male superiority on all sides ("the woman's place is in the home looking after her husband and children"). And the continuing double standard in sexual behavior perpetuates the secondary role of women, causing some still to think it slightly indecent for a woman to enjoy sexual intercourse.

The point is that in the courtship period men often rate their dates in terms of sexual favors, women inveigle tit-for-tat presents and social experiences from their partners. Furthermore, women tend to defer gratification by accepting an inferior nature and role, only to let the suppressed resentment surface later on—sometimes with a vengeance.

Much of the dishonesty that runs through the courtship routine could be weeded out, also, if people could get past the thought that they must be sweet and calm and reasonable at all times while courting, and would take the chance of meeting each other as real persons. Such a view does not deny the validity and force of certain romantic elements within the relationship. Infatuation and ideal expectations, in proportion, draw two people together and thus provide them the opportunity to do their further exploration. There may even exist between them a kind of vision of each other as "perfect," thereby calling forth new qualities in each other. But these feelings alone belong only to the realm of temporary pseudo love—harmless if they don't trap two people in an incompatible marriage web.

If a couple during courtship is able to reach the point where they are two equal people getting to know each other in all the behavioral areas of their lives, then they are free to negotiate the development of their behavior together. The question of sexual expression arises in this context. Respecting each other as persons, the two partners must decide together the extent of their intimate relationship. A relationship where sex is used to manipulate and coerce is obviously not one in which the couple confronts each other in honesty and respect. The needs and desires of both the man and the woman, including an expression of the kind of relationship they would like to explore and develop together, should be of primary consideration.

Perhaps the best word of caution is one by Robert Blood:

> When a couple start petting before they develop a close companionship, the sexual aspects of the relationship are likely to dominate it. When the relationship is basically sound, partial intimacy within the limits of both partners' convictions is more likely to strengthen and enrich it.[5]

On the other hand, some couples who are mutually committed to a genuine exploration of their relationship in all its dimensions may find that it is appropriate for them to include the sexual dimension in their premarital courtship pattern.

The sexual aspect of courtship, if not contained in a larger context, can provide such a disproportionate influence on the couple that their true vision of each other is distorted. Therefore it is very important for the couple to make an effort to discover the other facets of each other. What, indeed, do they talk about between periods of romancing?

On our Marriage Interview Schedule the respondents' answers to the question "How well did you know your partner before you were married?" ranged from 2½ months to 8 years, with most answers being about 1 or 1½ years. One particular answer did not specify in months or years but illuminated the experience of many people. A woman wrote: "Not as well as I thought I did, but reasonably well, as we have not

[5] Robert O. Blood, Jr., *Marriage*, 2nd ed. (New York: The Free Press [1962] 1969) ; p. 141.

27

had any serious problems because of not knowing each other. However, I think one always has a lot of getting to know each other to do *after* the wedding." It does, of course, take a long time to get to know someone, given all our pretenses and defenses. Yet the extent to which people come to know each other depends less on length of time than on degree of openness. If their lines of communication are open now for the expression of real feelings, they may well remain so.

In the final analysis, to choose a mate at all is to wager, since no one can know how he himself, or the partner, or the two of them together will develop. But insofar as feelings are intentional—pointing us to the future—we can take the risk of willing to be involved in the process of active loving: "We participate in the forming of the future by virtue of our capacity to conceive of and respond to new possibilities, and to bring them out of imagination and try them in actuality." [6] The ability to choose a life partner rests finally in trusting one's own feelings, trusting the other person to be open and willing to work in mutuality, and trusting the relationship to grow and mature without fear of change.

Courtship, then, can be the occasion for letting the emotion of sheer physical attraction expand to include a love of the whole person in relationship to oneself. But too often courtship is not used for such a purpose; the images and illusions stay intact and unrecognized differences become major problems later in the marriage.

MARRIAGE EXPECTATIONS—FOR BETTER OR WORSE

In considering the discrepancy between expectation and realization in marriage, let us focus our game of remembering it like it was on a third important area, namely, what the couple expected from marriage. The human capacity to antic-

---

[6] Rollo May, *Love and Will* (New York: W. W. Norton and Co., 1969), p. 92.

ipate is nowhere more rampant than in marriage. Just as what we meant when we said we were "in love" and how we subsequently conducted our courtship period have implications for the state of our marriage in middlescence, so also it is important to clarify our common expectations. People who enter marriage expecting too much or to little are bound for disappointment.

More than one person has had the experience of walking down the church aisle or into the office of the justice of the peace and discovering that the intended marriage partner has suddenly become a total stranger. If the person was able to refrain from absolute panic in the face of this sensation, he or she then no doubt found that the feeling passed and familiarity returned. To a certain extent this experience may ebb and flow throughout the life of the marriage, partly because of the ultimate mystery of each person, and partly because the tension between wanting to belong to someone and wanting to be free exists in all of us. Our love for someone entices us into a relationship which may threaten our freedom or alternately, be an open door of liberation. If our expectation is that of a deprived or lost freedom, then we may indeed fulfill a ball-and-chain prophecy by allowing this image to be a drag on marriage relationships.

In answer to a question about what he expected his marriage to be like, one of our respondents looked back across his seventeen years of wedded life to make the following observation:

> I remember that we used to think that we had to have a lot of things in common and we were expected to share each other's enthusiasm for their own hobbies, vacations, interest, etc. I was expected to develop more of an interest in politics and social action things and expected her to be a regular ol' buddy when it came to hunting, fishing, general outdoor enjoyment, etc. I gave up quicker than she did, realizing it was a stupid waste of her time and "What the

hell did I expect"—that's what cronies are for anyway, and I had them already.

Few people have the insight this man discovered early in his marriage and many remain continually frustrated because of the gap between promise and fulfillment. On the other hand, couples who were able to share every aspect of their lives together have later discovered, to the detriment of their marital relationship, that their interest was never really genuine or that such constant togetherness became suffocating.

What a person expects in his marriage is often reflected in his reasons for marrying, reasons deeper and more subconscious than the general response that a person marries because he "falls in love." At this deeper level there are many factors at work. People may marry out of loneliness (although it seems apparent that lonely people who marry other lonely people may remain lonely), or because of economic fears, or out of need for a parental symbol. They may marry simply because society expects it, an attitude enforced by people who regard middle-aged, single people with suspicion or pity. Many people marry because marriage seems to offer the best chance for fulfillment in life, including the establishment of a home and the bearing and rearing of children.

The sheer presence of sexual desire is, of course, a primary factor in drawing two people toward marriage. Where there is a firm belief that the satisfaction of sexual feelings must wait until after the wedding ceremony, a couple may marry in order to satisfy their sexual passion even though their better judgment tells them they are marrying the wrong persons.

There are many more reasons, conscious and unconscious, why people marry, but, when all of them have been examined, it is interesting to consider the simple conclusion reached by Doctors John Levy and Ruth Munroe in a book written thirty years ago.

People do not marry because it is their social duty to perpetuate the institution of the family, or because the preach-
er and Mrs. Grundy both recommend matrimony, or even
because they fall in love with each other. They marry because they lived in a family as children and still cannot
get over the feeling that being in a family is the only proper,
indeed only possible, way to live.[7]

While some young people today may not find this a compelling argument in their decision to marry, most of us will
recognize the validity of this observation. It is true that the
idea that we marry and establish a family because we once
lived in families as children is not very romantic, but this
is exactly why so many of our marital expectations are not
fulfilled.

Through the popular images reflected in our advertising,
our movies, and our novels we are frequently led to expect
that marriage would provide an eternally glowing romance.
One marriage counselor commented in a personal interview
that, generally speaking, the two major frustrations in marriage are the man's expecting the woman to be far more sexually responsive than she is, and the woman's expecting the
man to be far more romantic than he is. Their mutual feelings of frustration and disappointment often lead to other
feelings of disillusionment, and to the sense of being cheated
or of missing something through the years. It is the gap
between what they expect and what they experience that
causes many couples to feel their marriage is not successful.

This observation of the difference between the male and
female expectations in marriage has been borne out in a
recent study of middle-aged women made by psychologist
Clifford Rose Adams. Sex is number two in the man's list of
priorities for selecting a mate, while it is number six on the
woman's list. According to Dr. Adams, the subconscious fac-

[7] John Levy and Ruth Munroe, *The Happy Family* (New York: Alfred
A. Knopf, 1940), p. 3.

31

tors influencing the male in mate selection run as follows: companionship, sex, love-affection-sentiment (a single category), home and family, a helpmate, security. For the female the list of subconscious influences looks like this: love-affection-sentiment, security, companionship, home and family, community acceptance, sex. Dr. Adams concludes that this discrepancy cannot but lead to widespread dissatisfaction in marriage.

Other dimensions of conflicting expectations may be gleaned from the following case profile:

John and Sally have been married for twelve years and have finally decided to call it quits. Their hostility toward one another runs so deep that neither can find anything positive to say about the other. This was not the way it always had been. Their wedding, just after graduation, was a noteworthy social event. John had been a campus leader and football star at a large state university and during his senior year was selected by a national magazine to its "All-American Team." Sally came from a socially prominent family and had been a pretty and popular debutante. They were madly in love and had married after a brief courtship.

Although better known for his brawn than his brains, John had managed to gain admission to law school, perhap through the influence of his father, a prominent corporation attorney who had made substantial financial contributions to the school. During the years of professional study (and off and on later too), Sally worked in a bank to support the family, taking time off for the birth of two children. She received financial subsidy also from her parents. Meanwhile, John really had to struggle to keep up with his studies, and he found himself repeatedly on academic probation. He finally managed to graduate by stretching out his program and taking a lighter load. Even so, he was probably at the bottom of his class.

Upon graduation, John professed no interest in taking a job, explaining that he needed time to recuperate. Meanwhile, Sally continued to work to support the family and to raise the children as well. Financial subsidy now came from both sets of parents, who were visibly irritated by John's nonchalance. John, in turn, grew more resentful and stated that he hated his father. After nearly a year of loafing, John reluctantly took a position in a large law firm where he lasted about two years, after which he claimed he could not stand the "Mickey Mouse."

Another nonwork period followed, during which the seams of their marriage fell apart. Sally had lost her patience, and the couple engaged in violent arguments. Soon John joined a small law firm to work with a former classmate. On this job he seemed to get along better, but then after three years he finally claimed he just didn't feel up to it. After drifting for a while, John took on odd jobs as a janitor, cleaning up in banks and medical buildings. He seemed happy with his new work, for it left him with free time to work out on various athletic fields and to play with the neighborhood children who followed him like a pied piper. By this time, however, Sally had become thoroughly disgusted and began rejecting John, who in turn charged that Sally lacked sympathy and understanding.

In this thumbnail sketch of a marriage breakdown, it is obvious that Sally expected the best and felt she got the worst. She expected John to be a successful lawyer following in the footsteps of his father, but instead he was a misfit in the law profession. "I did not intend to marry a janitor," she sobbed. Sally expected a life of affluence, with membership in the country club and status in the community with her social set. Instead she had to struggle to make ends meet, became dependent upon parents for funds, and lost her self-respect vis-à-vis her debutante circle of friends. She thought she was marrying a winner and would be taken care of, but then she found herself being a part-time breadwinner and playing a more dominant role than the submissive one she had envisioned.

Fresh from being "Big Man on Campus," John entered marriage thinking he could tackle life much like he pursued victory on the gridiron. He set too high a goal for himself and, when the going got rough, didn't have the mental and emotional equipment to cope. He overreached and felt a sense of failure which immobilized him. The success image, together with his father's expectation, goaded him and lurked ominously in his psyche both at the conscious and unconscious level. Later on, he underreached in seeking out menial jobs. He knew he had failed to meet Sally's expectations, but this only served to induce a sense of guilt and shame and led to irrational outbursts and arguments between them. Their mutual expectations having been dashed, for better or for worse, it was too late to readjust common goals, given the repressed bitterness and hostility which now surfaced.

Thus far we have explored various facets of the marriage mystique in setting forth the situation of the spouse gap. Our intention has been to uncover some of the seeds of the problem even prior to marriage itself.

From this preliminary look at the mystique in marriage which leads people to fall in love, court, and commit their lives together, and the consideration of what they expected in that relationship, let us turn to look more concretely at some of the early gaps which inevitably appear shortly after the wedding ceremony.

II

CONFLICT: EARLY GAPS IN THE MARRIAGE-GO-ROUND

A magazine cartoon shows a young man in shirt sleeves in the doorway of an obviously suburban home, passionately kissing a woman wearing an apron and holding a cooking spoon. Two men in the yard next door are observing this tender scene, and one says to the other: "They're newlyweds. He just got back from putting the garbage out."

While few newlyweds are so inseparable, the cartoon does point up the sense of attachment during those early days of marriage that makes parting a poignant experience. One woman describes how tears would well in her eyes and a lump form in her throat as she watched her husband go down the stairs and off to work each morning after they were first married. Anniversaries are celebrated at every opportunity —at least they are not forgotten! This early period of sweetness and light when the honeymoon glow is still all-pervasive reveals the couple cuddling in the sheer ecstatic joy of belonging to each other.

Unfortunately, however, this euphoric state of dovesmanship does not last forever; in fact, it rarely lasts longer than the first few months after the wedding ceremony. The average American marriage begins to "settle down" almost from its inception. The spouses wake up from their blissful sleep after several months and find that the magic spell has been broken. It seems that the honeymoon represents the peak of the husband/wife relationship and from there marriage is lived in the valleys and shadows, with crevices and chasms creating gaps on all sides.

The sexual area is representative, perhaps, of this conflict. Couples usually begin their marriages with a high frequency of sexual intercourse, which then subsides with each passing month and year. The sex act loses its novelty as the availability of the partner is accepted, thereby diminishing its first intriguing, and almost forbidden, fruit. This loss of novelty and excitement is true of almost every aspect of the marital relationship and is a primary indicator that the couple are entering a new stage in their interaction.

At this point it is important for the couple to recognize the changing character of their life together. Too often the vow to "love, honor, and obey till death us do part" is interpreted as a static promise. In reality, however, the kind of trust that underlies this vow can only develop as the partners share, and clarify the meaning of, their mutual experiences over the course of time. Both the individual spouses and the marriage itself will be changing constantly. Unless the couple, by agreeing to care for each other "for better or worse," accept and accommodate this inevitable change, then the trust can never grow and the marriage will die as the initial bloom fades.

Someone, with tongue in cheek, has likened marriage, with its ups and downs to Wall Street: Each is a two-way street, filled with cracks and potholes and with unpredictable gains and losses, disasters and riches; each soars and sours, has highs and lows, peaks and valleys, good weather and storm —and also unexpected dividends. Carrying the metaphor a bit further, we may say that marriage cannot be sold short; for only as the spouses accept the changing moods and make an investment for the longer term can the bonds of marriage mature and capital gains be realized. Traders should stay out of the marriage market. It is strictly for the investor with an eye to the future.

Some marriages keep deteriorating until they verge on collapse in separation and divorce, while others manage to resist the process of decay; and in between these two poles are the many marriages in which couples stick it out together despite the fact that they have lost their first feelings of fascination and have been unable to find a fulfilling new basis for their relationship. If it is true, and we believe it is, that a mature and satisfying marriage is one that is nourished and that ripens, then the couple must develop a relationship capable of sustaining each of them through times of disenchantment with the spouse.

In the Prologue we described a basic rhythm in life that was utilized by the Greek dramatists, a rhythm which moved from purpose to passion (or suffering) to perception. When applied to the maturation of marriage the rhythm goes something like this: A newly married couple first enjoys a short, blissful period in which emphasis is on the mutual *enjoyment* of committing themselves to a common purpose; next the couple moves into a period in which emphasis is on mutual *adjustment* and they must work through differences and conflicts with whatever passion or suffering these may entail; then the couple is able to move in to a new period whose emphasis is on mutual *fulfillment* using the insights they have gained from their experiences together. Within this overall rhythm as it characterizes the whole marriage, of course, there will be many, repetitions of the same pattern as the couple confronts crises at either ultimate or mundane levels—occuptional changes, raising children, moving, friendships, finances, etc.

In this chapter we will focus on the second stage of this rhythm in an effort to pinpoint the early difficulties.

During the initial months and years together, a couple establishes certain patterns of interaction for problem-solving. How successful they are in dealing with early difficulties greatly affects their marriage later on when they hit the middlescent period. We invite you to join us in reconstructing the early days of your own marriage: First, when you really knew that the honeymoon was over; second, when dissatisfaction with reality in comparison with leftover romantic images and ghostly lovers arose; and third, when you capitulated to the daily routine of married life.

THE HONEYMOON IS OVER

The honeymoon is over
And we find that dining by candlelight
makes us squint
And that all the time
I was letting him borrow my comb and hang up his wet
 raincoat in my closet,
I was really waiting
To stop letting him.
And that all the time
He was saying how he loved my chicken pot pie,
He was really waiting
To stop eating it.
(I guess they call this getting to know each other.) [1]

Before long the charade and tact, diplomacy and discretion (that is, hypocrisy and dishonesty!) that characterized the courtship period give way to the necessity of expressing how we honestly feel about each other and the way we do things. We all recognize the trivial argument underlying the old marital conflict over whether the toothpaste tube should be squeezed from the top or the bottom. In the course of the dispute usually one spouse adds fuel to the fire with the dig: "That's a stupid thing to do." This kind of picky and seemingly petty difference of opinion can, if unexpected and unrecognized, be blown up all out of proportion—and, surprisingly, often is.

Behavior we could put up with on occasion becomes a monstrosity when faced day after day. The hobby that was so marvelous becomes a pain in the neck, the peculiar habit that was so cute becomes a screaming annoyance. All those

[1] From the poem "The Honeymoon Is Over," by Judith Viorst in her collection *It's Hard to Be Hip Over Thirty . . . & Other Tragedies of Married Life* (New York: New American Library Signet Book, 1970) , p. 19.

opposite qualities which attracted us to our partner in the first place, making him or her so charming, exciting, and interesting, begin to get on our nerves after a while and we start our efforts to make him (or her) over in our own image. In Clifford Odets' marvelously humorous and poignant story about the Flood, *The Flowering Peach*, Noah takes to God his exasperation with his family, saying, "People just won't stop acting like human beings!"

And so it is inevitable that gaps begin to appear early in the marital relationship. We may really feel it is important for each person to be allowed to be himself, but when being ourselves involves a contest over whether we sleep with the windows wide open or shut, or whether we always have eggs and cereal for breakfast, our good intentions may go by the boards. We may really have talked to each other about the necessity for being open and honest, but the first time that openness means criticism of mother-in-law, or of the way the roast is being carved, or why clothes drawers are always left open, the defenses usually go up and honest feelings thereafter are repressed. However trivial, adjustments must be made on every front or, we may say, in every room of the new home. In the bedroom, for instance, there may be the difficulty of learning to put up with someone else's snoring when we have been accustomed to snoring alone. In the bathroom we confront problems related to washing out the ring around the tub or leaving the seat up (or down) on the toilet stool. A new wife was reduced to tears when she started to run a bath and got her new hairdo soaking wet because her husband had neglected to change the handle from shower to tub! In the kitchen there are decisions about the kinds of foods to eat ("O no, not another TV dinner!") and about taking out the garbage. In the living room there is the television set to be shared (will it be baseball or the early movie?) and ashes that have been flicked on the coffee table or rug to be dealt with.

These seemingly silly and superficial problems are actually

points of probing for working out the deeper, emotional hang-ups concerning "closeness" and "separateness" in the marital relationship. Each partner must go through a learning experience concerning both himself and his partner, and he must be willing to express how he feels. Such expressions become very difficult if they are met with ridicule or rejection. To let ourselves be known as we are, to level with one another, is perhaps the greatest risk we take with others.

> It is, after all, those nearest to us who best know our weaknesses, who with full reason can reproach us for them. This is why so many couples play at hide-and-go-seek. They fear that conversation, by becoming more real, will open wounds to which they are most sensitive, wounds made all the more painful because they are inflicted by one's closest partner.[2]

On the other side of this conflict lies the relief, security, and comfort of being stark-naked to at least one person in life before whom we can take off our masks, shed our psychological fig leaf, and not have to pretend anymore. Such a relationship with a marriage partner can enable me to move more easily with others because someone knows my faults and still accepts me and cares for me, as well as frees me to realize my greater potential because I am not hung up on feeling guilty or stupid. But the achievement of this mutual acceptance takes understanding and patience, and a willingness both to modify behavior out of sensitive consideration of each other's needs and to compromise individual views out of respect for each other as persons.

Unless a conscious effort is made to ventilate and to keep talking out conflicts, the gaps (which inevitably open with each new adjustment) simply become wider and more fixed. If we were to identify the primary cause of the spouse gap problem it would be "breakdown in communication." This

[2] George L. Earnshaw, *Serving Each Other in Love* (Valley Forge, Pa.: Judson Press, 1967), p. 20.

breakdown should not be confused with what appears to be a lack of communication, because the unconscious and non-verbal signals are usually very plentiful. The problem with unspoken communication (apart from the well-aimed kick under the table for committing a dinner party *faux pas*) is that it is easily misunderstood—the message sent simply is not necessarily the one received. For instance, a wife may find herself increasingly upset over the way her husband handles their finances; he might be overly stingy or he might be an irresponsible spendthrift. She retaliates by being chronically unable to respond romantically in their sexual relationships. He, unaware of the money problem, may interpret her passive lack of erotic response as an indication she is frigid or that she is seeing another man.

Thus whether a couple likes it or not, or understands it or not, they do develop a system of interaction which can be observed by the outsider: who defers to whom, how each pricks the other's sore points, what is allowable in conversation or behavior and by whom, etc. A couple may be totally unaware of the evolution and presence of such a system, knowing only that one or the other feels uncomfortable or irritable or imprisoned, or that he or she can't get through to the spouse with any understanding.

All marriages have friction, at least at first, and the partners must go through the process of determining the nature of their relationship and arriving at a viable pattern of communication and interaction. Usually each partner begins by wanting the other to make all the concessions, and it remains difficult to reduce the friction. The conscious clash in forms of behavior are hard enough, but to them we must add also the whole complex of unconscious traits each one brings from the past.

At first blush the notion of how to fight fair with your spouse—"the intimate enemy"—appears as a put-on. But actually a very helpful school of psychotherapy has recently emerged under the leadership of George R. Bach, coauthor of *The Intimate Enemy!* [3] Working with the idea of "constructive aggression," Dr. Bach and his associates have devised ground rules for fighting fair in love and marriage, assuming that couples who know how to fight together are couples who will stay together. Hence spouses who go for marriage counseling receive instruction in the art of fighting properly. Of course, these training sessions do not teach judo or the art of manly defense. Rather the "combatants" participate in group encounter exercises and learn how to manage conflict and to facilitate the capacity for intimacy.

Often it is the underlying forces of different backgrounds, personalities, and childhoods which bring two people together in marriage—and then drive them apart. Much of the breakdown in communication can be traced to the cultural differences in the way things are labeled. Information exchanged may be culturally clear to one partner and entirely foreign to the experience of the other. Here is a case in point: One spouse has come from a family in which all the members were encouraged to blow up and let go with their feelings in big, emotional arguments and then forget about the incident entirely. To the other marriage partner such traumatic and explosive behavior was seen as a terrifying outburst, an unnecessary upset followed by callous and insensitive indifference to the feelings of others that could only result in permanent scars.

Furthermore, it is rare that the act of getting married will improve any prior personality difficulties an individual may have had. Denis de Rougemont asks the cryptic if not cynical question: "Inasmuch as when taken one by one most human beings of both sexes are either rogues or neurotics, why should they turn into angels the moment they are paired?" [4] Nervous tension, loneliness, neurotic anxiety, fear of failure —all these, and other problems we are heir to, will be com-

[3] George R. Bach and Peter Wyden, *The Intimate Enemy* (New York: William Morrow and Co., 1969).

[4] de Rougemont, *Love in the Western World*, p. 313.

pounded in marriage. If one partner has suffered severe deprivation in childhood, he or she may well make excessive demands on the other person and may appear chronically hostile. If, in turn, the other partner entered the marriage with little experience of the needs of the opposite sex, that very naïve ignorance will intensify the frustration of the first partner.

Sometimes, also, a couple coming from a pious background or attempting to found a home on religious principles will put a premium on being friendly, pleasant, agreeable, and harmonious to the point that conflicts are never surfaced, discussed, or resolved. Roy Fairchild points out that this attitude really rests on a mistaken interpretation of the very scripture the couple seek to affirm: "The exaggerated need for agreement and harmony in many of these homes has little in common with the New Testament view of life which speaks of alienation, reconciliation, and forgiveness, and definitely not of an ideal of living the mild, unending joy of conflictless existence." [5]

All close relationships demand a working out of conflicts between personalities, and certainly marriage is the most intimate and demanding of all. "Even the power of the sex and mating drives cannot overbalance the hostilities if the childhood pattern of either partner is too disturbed, if the pattern too far impairs the mature feelings or if the fit of the patterns between the partners is poor." [6] On the other hand, marriage is not a fixed and rigid stand-off relationship between two immovable and inflexible objects. The partnership allows for fluid interaction, for change, but such change can only come when it is recognized that there is a gap between the spouses' backgrounds and value systems causing conflict not previously

[5] Roy W. Fairchild, "Parental Stress in Protestant Homes: Clues from Research," *Sex, Family, and Society in Theological Focus*, J. C. Wynn, editor (New York: Association Press, 1966) , pp. 98-99.

[6] Leon J. Saul, *Fidelity and Infidelity* (New York: J. B. Lippincott, 1967,) p. 16.

known about. Then it is possible to radically minimalize the destructiveness of the gap.

Sometimes a couple may try to pretend that the honeymoon is not really over, trying to keep blissful ecstasy alive past the time when their relationship must appropriately change to another basis. Such pretense gives rise to the various games married people play in an attempt to maintain the desired illusions.

For instance, there is the game of "eternal romance" in which husband and wife say to each other, in essence, "You be my favorite date always." They continue to pretend that their connubial bliss is a sweet dream of sheer delight in spite of pressures, tensions, and mounting disillusionment. One wife in our survey reports that during the early years of marriage she showered and dressed up every afternoon to await her husband's return from work, as if her beau were coming to call. Most of us have experienced the person who boasts and brags about the spouse in public, citing the many talents waiting to be developed if only other people would give them an opportunity to be used. This kind of overprotective, oversolicitous attitude almost always masks a suppressed disappointment in the partner which is bound to erupt sooner or later—probably during the middlescent crisis.

Another marriage game is one we might call "complete fulfillment": Here a couple attempts to have their every need met within their relationship to each other, physical, psychological, intellectual, athletic, social, spiritual. Expecting to "make beautiful music together" forever and ever, the partners believe that they need no other resources. They may "let the rest of the world go by" and create their own private world. However, since it is rarely possible for one person to meet totally the needs of another over an extended period of time, the gaps will still appear and disillusionment will characterize the later stage of the game. Moreover, we have all known cases where the mutual dependence of one spouse upon the other is so total that the absence or death of one partner immobilizes the other.

A variation of this second marriage game is known as "we must be one." This game is based on the illusion that the marriage partners can share everything with each other and thus drive out all loneliness and feelings of separation. Each spouse gains fulfillment by possessing, and being totally possessed by, the other. Any conflict or attempt at privacy is automatically suspect since it seems to endanger the goal of "everything - that's - mine - is - yours - and - everything - that's - yours-is-mine." What here begins as an attempt to prevent gaps in the marriage ends by creating perhaps the most damaging gap of all, the estrangement resulting from overpossessiveness. A marriage, like any close relationship, can be choked by being held too tightly—squeezed to death in the name of togetherness. Better to let the honeymoon end and deal with the little inevitable gaps than to cling to the illusion that oneness can be free of conflict. In this case, what is held too tightly will be lost—in middlescence if not before—whereas what is held with open hands will allow life to flow into a free and changing relationship.

PHANTOM IMAGES AND GHOSTLY LOVERS

Sometimes our disillusionment with our marriage partners arises because they do not possess the admirable (and usually impossible) qualities or traits that we once ascribed to them. The tower of virtue we erected turns out to be a fragile figment of our own imagination, a paper-mache contrivance. Here the conflict is not so much the task of working out an agreeable system of communication once the honeymoon is over, but the result of an inability to see the other person as a real live flesh-and-blood reality. The gap appears with all its force and fury when illusion is shattered as the hard facts ineviably come to light.

We discussed some of the implications of romantic love in

the previous chapter. Now we will look at two particular instances of the gap such romantic or illusory love causes when it brings conflict in the early stages of marriage. One instance represents an "abstraction" of the romantic-love image called the Phantom Image; the other instance represents a "symbolization" of the romantic-love image called the Ghostly Lover.

Those who consider marriage to be the grave of love usually have a view of love as a kind of emotional infatuation, since infatuation inevitably fades as two people continually bump into each other in the daily round of living. They believe that marriage has killed the love which bloomed when the couple was free. Actually, this notion is characteristic of the experience in which love is built around a Phantom Image. Armed with feelings and images created for us by the songs and stories glorifying romantic love, we contrive, within our imaginations, an ideal person. This fantasy can become so vivid that we are then able to create it in the body of a person to whom we are attracted, attributing to that person certain highly desirable but actually nonexistent qualities. Then we cannot help being disappointed when we discover that the traits we thought were present in the other are not and never have been there at all. What we have done is enter into an unrealistic, dream relationship with a dream person whom we have fantasized in terms of our own needs and desires. The wish has fathered the thought. This Phantom Image is but a creation of our imaginations, an abstraction from our notions about romantic love and lovers.

Consider the case of Martin and Annette. Martin was the product of a broken home, having lived with his mother after she divorced his father when Martin was still a child. Martin remembers little about his father, who remarried shortly thereafter and moved across the country. He did, however, fantasize a great deal about his father and the new wife, seeing in their relationship all kinds of romantic and intriguing overtones. The boy had plenty of time for his dreams because his mother worked to help supplement her alimony and there were no brothers and sisters.

Martin's mother dated other men occasionally as her son was growing up, then she married again when Martin was in his last year of high school. Whereas the mother and son had been quite close, Martin found himself having to share her with this new man. Bedroom doors were now closed, and Martin began to fantasize about his mother and her new husband in much the same way he had about his father.

Uncertain what to do with himself, Martin joined the service after graduation and was sent overseas to Korea. Daydreams, movies, and romantic novels helped him endure the loneliness of the experience, and he fantasized elaborate pictures of finding the right girl with whom he would have the kind of happiness he felt each of his parents had discovered. While overseas Martin did a lot of dating and had his first sexual experiences. These gave him confidence in his manhood, but he felt no respect for the girls who were partners in his affairs and never considered marrying any of them.

When Martin was discharged from the service he was ready and eager for a real romance. Within a few months he met a childhood friend named Annette who had been ill for quite a long time with mononucleosis, and who was also ready to date. Annette's parents knew Martin's mother and they attended the same church. Martin also respected Annette, who was a virgin and felt strongly about "saving herself for the man she married." Immediately they fell in love, experiencing misery when separated even for a day, and they rushed headlong into marriage.

Martin saw Annette as a frail beauty in need of protection, who was sensitive to his every mood and need, the "ideal woman." Annette saw Martin as a man of the world in whom still waters ran very deep, the "ideal man." However, the two of them started having trouble on their honeymoon, for Martin found himself frustratingly impotent with his new bride and Annette was fearfully homesick. They separated a short time later and then divorced, both of them bewildered and sadly disillusioned.

What Martin and Annette failed to realize is that they had been in love with their Phantom Images—in love with love, and in love with themselves in love. They mistook superficial similarities for qualities for making a perfect match together, even unconsciously avoiding any discussions which would in any way shake their illusions. Both of them dreamed so much about being in love that they projected their ideal images onto each other. It would have been impossible for either one to fulfill the fantasy.

Another example of the person looking for a Phantom Image is the figure of the Don Juan. For this man the excitement of love is in the search for and conquest of the ideal woman, but always the image fades upon conquest and he must start searching again. He feeds on the image of himself as devoted to the cause of true love. Such an image can only be maintained as an illusion, however, for to actually see Don Juan as a real person would destroy the thrill and magic of his romantic intrigue. Alas, Don Juan remains as a dashing literary figure. As a living person he would doubtless be an insufferable egomaniac.

Just as an active imagination can produce a Phantom Image to love, so also a person can project from deep within an image of his or her "other half" onto a real or imaginary person of the opposite sex and create what has been called a Ghostly Lover. This rather complex psychological process has been particularly illuminated through the insights of Carl Jung and his followers. Each person has both a masculine and a feminine side to his nature, with one or the other being dominant and thus representing the sex of the individual. The whole and healthy person recognizes both sides of himself and integrates them into himself in their proper balance. The masculine side of the woman is called her *animus* and the feminine side of the man is called his *anima*.

When a man and woman meet, it is possible for either or both to project on the other party certain elements from this unconscious anima or animus, causing immediate attraction or repulsion. We should note in passing that it is possible also for the man or woman to respond to such a projection by emphasizing what the other wants to see. An example of this is seen in the woman who becomes soft and pliant, sensitive and responsive toward a man she loves, then is as surprised as he is when, after their marriage, she finds she becomes domineering and has definite ideas about things which previously she deferred to his decision.

Usually these projected fantasies become tempered in reality by real friendships and interaction. Sometimes, however, there is a tendency to cling to the world of dreams, particularly when outer contacts are not easily made or an early attachment is cut off for some reason. A young girl, for instance, may take refuge in a fantasy world where there is a suitor who plays his role as she would like it, becoming her Ghostly Lover, an image which then stands between her and all other males she meets. It is likely, as the girl grows up that the Ghostly Lover will become buried in her unconscious and she will think no more about him, but he may still reside within her as the "beau ideal" against whom all other attractions fall short.

The trouble with a Ghostly Lover is, of course, that he represents an impossible possibility, a reach always beyond grasp. The values the woman projects onto him cannot exist in terms of a living relationship to a man. Preoccupation with such a fantasy draws her away from life into a kind of spirit-world communication, removed from reality. This phenomenon has been described in some detail by Mary Esther Harding in her book *The Way of All Women:*

As Ghostly Lover he always acts as one who lures his victim away from reality by promises of bliss in another world. In the woman's psychology he is the counterpart of the Siren in the man's. In the man's psychology, as in mythology, the Siren by her music and charm lures the man to a watery grave. The Ghostly Lover, by the promise of untold bliss, entices the woman to seek his arms in the air.[7]

Experience with a Ghostly Lover has been the subject of a number of plays and novels. In the legend of the Dybbuk, made into a drama by Solomon Rappaport, the ghost of a dead youth enters a girl whom he loved and lives with her in her subjective world. Eugene O'Neill's play *Strange Interlude* deals with a girl who loved a young man killed in the war. Though the girl marries, her real devotion is to her lost lover; She can give nothing of herself to life because her soul belongs to her ghostly fantasy. Then there is J. M. Barrie's play *Mary Rose,* in which a girl is lured by strange music away from her husband and child to the Island-that-wants-to-be-visited. In all these works the Ghostly Lover is a projection of unconscious forces resting deep within the person herself.

If one spouse clings to the precious memory of a Ghostly Lover, it can make life ghastly for the other partner. One of our interviewees, David, reported with candor that his first real quarrel with his wife took place in the early months of marriage. It seems that David, try as he might, could not blank out of his mind the memory of Carol, a high school sweetheart with whom he carried on a torrid love affair before going off to college. David kept faithfully in touch with Carol, but after a year or so he was shocked to receive word that his beloved had married someone else. He never could quite get over the heartbreak. Even after his marriage to Eileen the memory of Carol lingered to haunt the relationship. During sexual intercourse with Eileen, the vision of Carol kept crossing his mind until finally, on one occasion, he inadvertently blurted out the name Carol. Eileen was furious and claimed that David didn't really love her.

[7] (New York: Longmans, Green and Co., 1933) , p. 44.

There is probably an element of animus-anima projection in the love of all men and women when they marry. After the glamour has started to fade in the couple's early months together, each begins to realize that the other does not really see him as he is. The gap has opened between illusion and reality. If the gap leads to conflict and remains unresolved, the couple may give up and separate. If the gap is glossed over the misconceptions allowed to go unchallenged, the Ghostly Lover may surface in the unconscious providing his judgmental comparisons: the wife may eventually find herself imagining her husband to be someone else when he makes love to her; the husband may fantasize a companion to fill his commuting hours to and from work; and both may become vulnerable to the presence of attractive strangers on whom they can project their ghosts.

If, on the other hand, the first gap is recognized, the couple can consciously seek out the projections each has made and can establish some beachheads of true relatedness. Over the years reality and understanding can then take the place of illusion.

One final word on the subject of fantasy. We all bring into our relationships images of ourselves as well as the image of the person we want to love. Many times we don't like ourselves very much and are awestruck when we discover that someone actually loves us. Suddenly our self-image changes, and we experience a transformation of that old self into a new one by the power of that love. But shades of Phantom Images and Ghostly Lovers! That excitement does not last forever either. Thus Levy and Munroe point out another kind of gap we must confront during those early months of marriage:

> Our disillusionment does not proceed wholly, or perhaps even primarily, from the unromantic facts we learn about our partner in the course of daily observation. It comes largely from our bored recognition of the same old self

51

within our own breast. Our own newfound charm and prowess and glamour evaporate when we can no longer read them in a worshipping gaze, when we are no longer stimulated by the desire for conquest.[8]

Such a recognition can be an occasion for flight to new illusions or for hanging in to build some kind of real self-understanding—with the help of the partner who is doing the same thing.

BECOMING ROUTINELY MARRIED

So the honeymoon is over, the illusions have been shattered, and now the couple settles down to the routine of being married. Remember the way it was during those early years? Remember all those mundane and do-or-die activities, projects, and concerns that held you and your spouse together despite the sparks they sometimes ignited?

Perhaps one or both of you was still in school when you married and you had to budget your time and energies to include classes and papers and final exams. Or perhaps you both worked, shared the housekeeping tasks, and looked forward to the day the wife could quit working and you could start a family. During those days you probably talked a lot about career aspirations and job opportunities, and about saving money. Then you began to invest in capital goods. You bought a house, furniture, appliances, a new car (all duly financed), and you faced the problems of mortgages and credit card payments. You also built up a social life, making friends, entertaining, joining groups, etc.

Next the routine was probably interrupted, reorganized, and set in motion again around a new center of attention, the arrival of your first child. Further time and attention were demanded by the baby, both from the mother, who had the immediate care, and from the father, who sought to en-

[8] Levy and Munroe, *The Happy Family,* p. 67.

sure proper support. All in all, there was little leisure in those early years to deal with the subtler aspects of life, including conscious reflection on the changing needs of the individual partners.

This doesn't mean that conflict or difficulty were absent from those days. The woman (even though she may never have heard of Betty Friedan) doubtless spent many hours in resentment at being a "trapped housewife" whose only company was children or other trapped wives, and in feeling that her mind was atrophying. Imagine the frustration of the housewife who, having been told in college that she was an intelligent and creative human being, now finds her conversation confined to babies and detergents! Some women may have adjusted to the demands of home and family by becoming compulsive housekeepers, others by becoming activist mothers or neighborhood gossips. And of course all wives turned to their husbands for help and support the minute they arrived home from work during those "witching hours" when everyone is demandingly hungry and the children are screaming for attention and the roast is burning in the oven.

The man, on the other hand, spent his days fighting the commuter traffic, handling competitors at work, doing business over lunch, joining the rat race, surviving in the "jungle," or simply putting in his time at some unchallenging task, arriving home pooped, if not always proud. One author describes the man who discovered that the dark night of the soul came not at 3:00 in the morning but about 5:30 P.M. on the commuting train for home: "A hard day at the office *versus* a hard day on the home front, each combatant waiting to tell his story first, to enlist the sympathy so rightly deserved." [9]

Despite the obviously petty and pedestrian activities, the

* Robert N. Rodenmayer, *I John Take Thee Mary* (Greenwich, Conn.: Seabury Press, 1962) , p. 69.

daily routine of the marriage-go-round does unite a couple during those early years of marriage in an extraordinary way through their sheer lack of time and energy to attend to all the deeper personal difficulties and conflicts. At the same time, however, patterns of interaction do continue to evolve within the marriage which have far-reaching implications for the general spouse-gap situation. We will explore four areas which are representative of this pattern of interaction.

First, the couple must arrive, consciously or unconsciously, at the establishment of some kind of decision-making process. This may be done on an authoritarian basis (one spouse is subservient and acquiesces to the other), or in terms of a kind of verbal coercion (one spouse convinces the other to accept his decision), or through mutual discussion. This third method would involve the couple in determining together such questions as what they want, how they will get it, and who will do it.

Perhaps the main difficulty in achieving an agreeable system for determining rules and responsibilities is the tendency of a new couple to try to base their patterns on what they think is a normal or conventional model. There is, in fact, no such thing as a "normal" marriage, and behavior patterned on other marriages will likely fail because each person and each couple has different needs and abilities. Furthermore, what appears to be a desirable relationship among friends or family members may not really be so underneath. Efforts to assign responsibilities on the basis of what society thinks appropriate for each sex rather than on competence and interest is also a breeding ground for trouble. Lederer and Jackson tell of a very satisfying marriage between the owner of a hardware store and an active Vassar College graduate. In the late afternoon he cooks dinner while she works in the garden and does repair jobs around the house. Society would say this is unconventional, but the truth is he dislikes gardening and is tired of tools by the end of the day, but he is an excellent chef; she is a mediocre cook, but is a skilled gardener and handywoman! [10]

The point is that the nature of the rules and responsibilities the couple decides on will greatly affect the degree of satisfaction each partner feels about the marriage, and thus will determine a great deal about the character of their relationship and interaction in middlescence.

Second, the couple must face the fact of conflict itself and determine how to deal with it when it arises. Most of us shy away from disagreements because they appear as threats to our relationship. Furthermore, most of us have been conditioned from childhood to think it is wrong to feel anger at someone we love or are supposed to love. Usually, then, when we feel anger we feel guilty and we repress both feelings, which then leads to even more repressed hostility until we get ulcers or headaches, or until some little thing sets us off in a tailspin. The responses to the question about settling arguments on our Marriage Interview Schedule revealed a strong indication that those who first argued and then quietly talked things out to some kind of resolution were the ones who generally felt happiest in their marriages. Those who never quarreled because it hurt the other person's feelings, or who gave up before reaching an agreeable compromise, continued to have feelings of frustration and tension in other areas of their relationship as well.

One thing which seems clear about quarrels is that when they erupt over something trivial they are frequently pointing to some deeper difficulty, for example, the husband who blew up at his wife for a minor driving error actually had been building up resentment for months over her reluctant attitude toward sex. Such suppression of negative feelings may give a semblance of marital harmony, but at a huge cost to the development of the relationship. Consider the young man and woman who love each other, marry, and come up

[10] Lederer and Jackson, *The Mirages of Marriage,* p. 18.

against their first major conflict. She, believing she must make her husband happy at all cost, represses her hurt and greets him with a smile. He, seeing her smiling face, thinks it must not be so bad after all and represses his hurt. The trouble blows over, and each attributes the difficulty to his own bad temper. Each time trouble recurs the two again repress their feelings. In time (if they stay together!) they learn self-control and tolerance, but they will remain strangers to each other and to themselves, as far as how they feel at their deepest levels of meaning. Without conflict, obviously one cannot know reconciliation.

The primary consideration in terms of marital adjustment is not really whether spouses quarrel, but why they quarrel and how they handle it. To be able to say what one has to say at a particular moment is indication that the wife or husband trusts the spouse and the marriage enough to be honest and to withstand the consequences. In the long run this trust pays off. Each partner asserts himself as an individual with real feelings who chooses to hang in with his mate and hammer out a life together, rather than simply acquiesce out of fear. The way quarrels are handled in the early years of marriage has obvious implications for the middlescent couple and will be dealt with later.

Third, the couple must come to terms with how they will relate at the most intimate level of their marriage, their sexual relationship. We return to this aspect of marriage, since it is so frequently mentioned by our respondents. We hear a lot about this gap these days and there is an implication that it is the most serious area of all. The interesting thing to note here is that, while sex is certainly a very important part of the couple's life, sexual adjustment may not be primary in determining the couple's satisfactory or unsatisfactory interaction. If other areas are working all right, the likelihood is that sexual relationship will be positive, but if there are problems elsewhere, there is often trouble in the bedroom. What happens is that when there is difficulty a couple can focus on sex as an identifiable source and sometimes as a scapegoat for their frustration and hostility.

Frequently a couple will try to move too fast in achieving mutual sexual satisfaction early in marriage. David Reuben's recent, popular, best-selling book *Everything You Always Wanted to Know About Sex* puts such overeagerness in its proper perspective. Copulation, Reuben says, is certainly not the transporting, idyllic experience that is pictured in contemporary literature, movies, or television, and will be disappointing to those who approach it with such expectations. He goes on to say that sex is tempered by the same less-than-perfect qualities that affect any human activity, and that "expecting too much guarantees disappointment." [11] How many couples have been inadequately prepared for their sexual relationship so that sheer ignorance creates a gap which counseling and common sense and reading can bridge with ease? How often does a wife actually fake an orgasm, taking a leaf from the celebrated notebook of the professional prostitute, and derive secret delight from her deception of having put across a fast one? How many couples are overly concerned about whether their sex relations are "normal"? Here as elsewhere, experience shows that conventional standards have little effect on a successful relationship. The couple must find what is mutually satisfying and rewarding to the two of them and to their marriage. An unhappy couple frantically experimenting to try to solve their problems, for instance, may have a higher frequency of intercourse than a couple whose experience is a genuinely happy one.

The sex gap is best met as husband and wife learn the language of sex and communicate through giving and receiving pleasure in that act of love. As the grinding pressures of the daily routine make inroads into their marriage, the

[11] David R. Reuben, *Everything You Always Wanted to Know About Sex*—*But Were Afraid to Ask* (New York: David McKay Co., 1969), p. 112.

couple may have to consciously create occasions for their love-making, for the desire is not always automatic and needs to be aroused. Unless the partners attend to that necessity, an important area of their communication and shared intimacy can be lost. The effect of the loss of this physical closeness and responsiveness becomes profoundly evident during middlescence.

Fourth and last (though not least!), the couple in early marriage must arrive at an understanding of their use of money. Mundane and unromantic as it sounds, money is indeed the root of much evil and contention in marriage. One probation officer observed after long years of involvement in domestic court cases, "You can sum up the cause of most marriage problems . . . under three headings—sex, in-laws, and money. And, if you ask me, I'd say money was the most common cause of all." [12]

Sometimes one spouse or the other has immature or unrealistic attitudes toward the earning and saving, or spending, of money. There is a cartoon showing a wife talking earnestly to her husband, saying, "If we put off paying the rent this month, and don't license the car, we'll be able to make a down payment on a refrigerator." Or, sometimes one spouse will use money as an emotional weapon to control or punish the other. This latter case is often true when the husband works and the wife does not. Unless the wife is given a personal allowance which she can spend as she chooses with no questions asked, her self-respect is greatly threatened and her extreme dependence on her husband can cripple their relationship.

Surely it is an understatement to say that the Women's Liberation Movement has yet to develop a beachhead in Japan, traditionally known as a "man's world." Wives in Lotus Land are typically referred to as *Oksan,* which literally

[12] David R. Mace, *Success in Marriage* (Nashville: Abingdon Press, 1958), p. 53.

translated means "that property," "that thing I own in the kitchen." A woman's chief goal in life is to serve her husband. And yet, with this attitude of deference on the part of women to the "master" of the house, it is typical for a Japanese husband to hand over his entire paycheck or envelope to the care of his *Oksan.* Clever, these Japanese women!

The attitudes a couple develop in relation to money will carry over into other decisions, and the way they handle their money is often an indication of the health (if not the wealth) of their marriage. Spending habits frequently reflect experiences with the previous patterns of parents and must be examined on the basis of the new relationship in the person's own marriage. Thus a spouse who was financially deprived as a Depression child may spend lavishly, and pamper and overindulge her own children, who are now growing up in an age of affluence. Traditionally the man has handled the family's finances, assuming that the woman has no head for figures, when actually she may be more adept, have more time, and like doing it better than he. The couple must determine together their roles and responsibilities on the basis of competence and interest. If both partners level with each other in the earning and spending of their money, the gap will be more easily bridged and the decisions put where they properly belong, in making the best use of their financial resources to make possible the life they want to live. If not, the gap created by conflicts over money may persist long past the time when the couple needs to worry about budgets and savings programs.

Let us say again that conflict in marriage is inevitable. The first gaps will appear between lovers in spite of all efforts to pretend otherwise. But this is not the end of the marriage drama, it is only the beginning—the first act, so to speak. How the couple has dealt with the end of honeymoon bliss, with the initial disillusionment of living with a real person, and with the complex problems inherent in the routine of the daily marriage-go-round, will, to a large degree, determine the way they interact in middlescence.

On, now, to a look at the monster itself—middle age—and what marriage turns into when it is a couple of decades old.

III

COMPLICATION: MIDDLESCENT MALAISE

As the curtain rises on the second act, we are immediately faced with a major complication within the story: the central characters have become middle-aged. While we knew this was bound to happen, it still comes as a surprise to learn that middlescence has dealt a staggering blow to the growth and development of the well-made marriage. The setting for this stage is one of upheaval, confusion, and suffering, reappraisal of who we are and where we're going. We have "remembered it like it was"; now we must "face it like it is."

No one is quite sure just where to locate the boundaries around middle age, and any age grouping in the life cycle is somewhat arbitrary. In answer to the question "When does middle age begin?" these distinguished citizens shed the following light:

> Leo Rosten, creator of H*Y*M*A*N K*A*P*L*A*N—"When all the policemen look young."
> Whitney Young, the late executive director of the National Urban League—"When the steps get steeper and the print gets smaller."
> C. James Miller, a neighbor in San Anselmo, California, and former college tennis star—"When your son starts licking you consistently on the tennis court."
> John Lindsay, mayor of New York City—"I'll let you know when I get there." [1]

[1] The above quotes are mainly from "The Pleasures and Perils of Middle Age," *Time*, July 29, 1966, p. 50.

The most all-inclusive description of middle age is probably the one by Harrison Smith who calls it "an increasingly elastic expanse between youth and old age."

Middle age is not simply a biological or even a demographic concept. "Two ideas stand out about the concept of middle age," Thomas Mayer points out, "Its inherent ambiguity and its inherent ambivalence. The ambiguity exists because middle age is defined by what it is between rather than on its own grounds. The ambivalence stems from the conflicting valuation placed upon being middle-aged." [2]

We usually associate middle age with certain revealing physically characteristics: the loss or greying of hair, the receding hairline, the deeper lines in the face, the wrinkled skin, the need for false teeth, bifocal glasses and/or hearing aids, the decline in muscular coordination, the loss of physical stamina, the expanding girth, the losing battle of the bulge against those extra pounds of flesh—the "spare tire" or the "bay window"—that we have a tendency to acquire. Try as we may to comb our hair every which way, the balding spots just seem to shine through.

A person realizes he has entered the period of middlescence when he finds himself preoccupied with matters of health, success, and sexual potency. Or he may experience a loss of interest in his work as well as a loss of faith in his abilities. He may find it hard to concentrate and make decisions, may become cranky and bored or irritated with his spouse. He may drink and smoke more while enjoying it less. He may lust after extramarital affairs.

Many women in middle age fear that they are losing the fetching attractiveness which once characterized them in bygone years. This was the case with Charlotte, a prominent lady in the community who unraveled a story about how she had gotten involved in a love affair with a minister. She was married to a prominent lawyer and was herself very active in

[2] Thomas Mayer, "Middle Age and Occupational Processes: An Empirical Essay," *Sociological Symposium*, Fall 1969, p. 89.

civic activities, but she had somehow gotten hooked up with this pastor for several years. The clergyman had recently begun to see the light, realizing that the end of the affair was inevitable. He proceeded to get psychiatric counseling which led him to the conclusion that he had to break off this relationship. That became the occasion for Charlotte's sadness and despair. She blamed the church, the clergy, this man, her husband, and fate itself. When asked why she had gotten involved with the clergyman in the first place, she answered: "I'm in my early forties now and I began to feel that I was losing my attractiveness. I had to prove to myself that I was not fading away but was still attractive to somebody important, so I took up with him."

An anxious fear that time is running out, a vague sense of mental or moral ill-being, a churning sense of self-doubt and disbelief, a general uneasiness at being in the afternoon of life—these are some of the symptoms which are inherent in the experience we call the middlescent malaise.

The middlescent is perhaps the most neglected of all age groups in America. Yet it is not stretching the imagination to claim that the one-fourth of the population between 35 and 55 actually occupy the seats of power, foot the bills, and make the decisions that affect how the other three-fourths live. Unrivaled in purchasing and political power and prestige, middlescent man rides the saddle of society. Like it or not, he manages the "Establishment." When the Power Structure and the Establishment are being attacked and pilloried, it is the middlescent who absorbs the blows. By and large, middlescents are not at war with the "system." They do not wish to bury it. The system is not for burning.

The average age of the labor force is 45, and the average of the men who run our businesses and government is around 50. During these years the married couple shoulders the greatest number of responsibilities they will ever have to face as they maintain the home, finish educating the children, deal with aging parents, meet increasing social and occupational obligations, provide for future economic independence, and attend to personal physical and mental fitness. The earlier growing pains of life and family seem minor compared with the gigantic issues which now face the middlescent couple, including the approaching or present experience of the menopause, the climacteric and generalized feeling of depression. There is the story of the twenty-year-old daughter who came in tears to see her forty-plus-year-old mother, telling how recent experiences in her new marriage had left her tense, anxious, and shaken. Her mother replied with some weariness, "Don't worry, dear, you're just going through a mini-pause."

Thus the most turbulent time of life seems to be neither adolescence, when time is measured from birth forward, nor senescence, when time is measured from death backward. It is middlescence, the in-between time, when there seems to be no time at all.

But the real problem facing the middle-age group is not an actual decline in usefulness, as many fear. It is, rather, the sense of ambivalence, the defeatist and antagonist attitude they and others have about being middle-aged. This stems, of course, from the fact that we are a child-oriented culture, in which the virtues of youth are celebrated and their fads and fashions avidly imitated. "As far as J. C. Penney's marketing is concerned," said the president of the department store, "nobody in this country is over thirty." The extent to which our nation sees youth as the hope of the future is implied in a paradoxical remark someone once made about "our venerable young!" In many other cultures age is highly esteemed as the fountainhead of wisdom—in the United States age is dismissed as embarrassing and a drag.

Only recently, perhaps, in the light of campus disorders, drug use, mammoth rock festivals, society dropouts, and general rebellion against the establishment has the youth subculture increasingly alienated the older generation. But the result has been a general hardening of the middle-aged into a more conservative position, thereby polarizing the generation gap even more. Many middle-agers have become resentful and envious of the pampered young who seem to have everything but gratitude. Perhaps the current crises may bring us someday to a more balanced perspective on the contribution each age group makes to the cultural life.

In the meantime, most of our attention continues to be focused on the young, with their needs and activities exploited for commercial reasons through a constant exposure in public print and on television. Not long ago the *Louisville Courier-Journal* published a marvelous piece on the way TV ads contribute to the demoralizing of adults by implying that nothing good can happen to anyone over twenty-five. The article goes on to suggest that when we watch the people portrayed in the advertisements for a while, a humiliating message comes through loud and clear:

 teenagers always have bright, glistening teeth, while adults have dentures and denture breath;

 young people have fun at amusement parks and beach parties, as older people go to movies and get nagging headaches or upset stomachs;

 the youthful wife makes a cup of coffee that turns her husband into a sex maniac, but the middle-aged wife spends all day washing, mopping, and ironing only to have her husband come home tired and cross with aching muscles, hay-fever allergy, and Excedrin headache number 57;

 the youth cult wears sneakers and sandals, has fun, and laughs even with their mouths full of hair, but the older generation wears support hose and girdles and has constipation, tired blood, and insomnia.

The article ends with the observation "It isn't fair. Worse, we have a feeling that it's all too true."

We commonly think of adolescence as a period of rapid

change, but when we stop to examine it, middlescence is likewise characterized by physiological and psychological change. For many these changes are cataclysmic. If you want an experience of culture shock, go to a high school reunion twenty years after graduation and note that you hardly recognize some of your old classmates. You would not want to say so right then and there, but after you get home and talk about the event it often seems comical: handsome, athletic Jack is now rotund and balding; popular, vivacious Dolores is now frazzled, plump, and drinks too much; liberal, risqué Harold is now a tired, jaded businessman and a conservative son of a bircher. You wonder with horror what *they* may be saying about you!

In addition to these obvious changes in appearance, middlescence is characterized also by a general anxious feeling that one needs to change one's life-style—change friends, change jobs, change homes, and, for some, even change (or exchange) wives. The housewife who has been down in the dumps for days, unable to decide whether to wear her red dress or her blue dress, whether to fry or barbeque the chicken, may suddenly begin rearranging the furniture or even buying a whole new set of furniture for the house. There is a strong, deep-seated compulsion, as it were, to change everything—not radical political or social change, which seems too far-out, but personal, manageable change that will hopefully satisfy the vague feeling of anxiety and dread.

Various studies reveal that the middle years are the peak years when income and productivity come to an apex. Of course there are hazards of the peak position—the fear of "peaking out," the prospect of a forthcoming downhill slide, the frustration born of the realization that one has hit a ceiling and can go no further. The peak experience is surely a high point. But just beyond the peak is where morale is tested and strained by a fear of decline and displacement.

In this chapter we will take a closer look at some of these manifestations of the middlescent malaise, the complications that put obstacles in the path of our happiness and well-being. The impact of the malaise on the marital relationship will be discussed in the following chapter. With as much objectivity as you can muster, we invite you now to "face it like it is" and explore with us these areas: (1) the middle-age squeeze between the concerns of the young and the difficulties of the aged, Invisible and Indispensable; (2) the impulse to review and judge one's life and work, Reviewing the Balance Sheet; (3) the debilitating effect of widespread boredom, Bore, Boring, Bored; and (4) the shock of facing one's lost youth, Trauma of Lost Youth.

INVISIBLE AND INDISPENSABLE

The middle-aged person is, literally, the person caught in the middle who must care for the old and accommodate the new generation. Middle-agers are required to be active in attempting solutions to the problems on both sides. Meanwhile, the middlescent himself is not expected to have any problems (and, indeed, he has little time left for his own!). He is supposed to be wiser than the young and stronger than the old. He is expected to be "responsible" at all times, while the antics of the young and the childishness of the old can be winked at.

One doctor noted that since most writers are very prolific during their middle years they have been concerned with everyone else's problems but their own. So middle-agers generally attract little attention and inspire few learned treatises. Scholarly research as well as public interest in the life cycle has centered almost exclusively either on childhood and adolescence, or on the elderly. Many studies and public programs deal with youth or with gerontology. But who speaks for middlescent man? In this sense he is forgotten and invisible within society. Like *The Invisible Man* immortalized by Ralph Ellison, the middlescent is ignored, neglected, and taken for granted. He is in danger of becoming a "lost generation." But insofar as both the young and the old lean on him for support, middlescent man is also indispensable. A recent *Time* article devoted to the plight of the aged in America called attention to this fact:

> For the "command generation" there are two generation gaps, and the decisions to be made about their parents are often more difficult than those concerning their children. . . . A difficult decision of the middle-aged is how to allot their resources between children and parents and still provide for their own years of retirement, which may well extend for two decades.[3]

It is little wonder that down-in-the-dumps depression is cited as the leading mental disorder among the middle-aged. No wonder middlescents regard themselves as the put-upon and stepped-on generation. Middlescents are getting tired of footing the bills and getting kicked in return. Thus far no "Middlescent Liberation Movement" has emerged. Yet the signs of a middle-aged rebellion should come as no surprise. "Middlescents unite! You have nothing to lose but your receding hairlines."

Let us look at some of the problems of being an in-between generation as we cite the concrete case of Barbara and Allen.

Barbara was twenty and Allen twenty-five when they married in 1946. They had met two years earlier through a mutual friend when Allen was home on leave from the army during World War II. Their correspondence flourished, and shortly after Allen was discharged they had a big church wedding and settled down in a university housing community where Barbara worked as a library assistant and Allen finished work on a degree in business management. The early years were financially difficult, especially after their

---

[3] "Growing Old in America," *Time*, August 3, 1970, p. 53.

first child, Mary, was born a week after their first anniversary. But they were also very happy—the war was over, they had found each other, and someday they would be realizing all their dreams for security and for a home in the suburbs full of happy, healthy children.

After graduation Allen was hired by a large mutual fund corporation as assistant personnel manager and he started up the ladder of promotions, finally becoming vice-president in charge of investment policies for one of the company's fifty million fund portfolios. Barbara was able to stop work for good after the second child, John, was born and became a devoted mother and wife, active in the usual social and charitable groups. She often went with Allen on business trips, leaving the children with grandparents.

Today we discover that Allen and Barbara are able to maintain a very comfortable life in affluent surroundings. But, at the present time, both their children and their parents are demanding emotional and financial support that Allen and Barbara had not anticipated. The situation with the children, for instance, runs something like the following.

The oldest daughter, Mary, is now twenty-three, has been married two years to a young man she met in college who is now in graduate school. They have just had their first baby and are hard pressed to make ends meet, since Mary is unable to work as a teacher at the moment. Barbara and Allen, remembering similar rough days of their own, try to help them out without intruding on the young people's sense of pride: a new car for their wedding, a washer and dryer one Christmas, baby furniture, and so forth, as well as periodic gifts of money made under some pretext about discovering a forgotten savings bond or an insurance refund.

John, the oldest boy, now twenty-one, has always been a bright, eager student who decided in high school to study law. Two years ago, however, John got caught up in the college student revolution and "blew" his junior year as far as studying was concerned. He then took a year out, continuing to be active both in radical campus politics and in the draft resistance, earning money by writing articles and doing odd jobs. John has now decided not to finish college, but to work for an underground newspaper. Barbara and Allen are terribly disappointed that John has not finished college, and feel miles apart from him in terms of goals and philosophy. It is difficult for them to understand his far-left political views, which seem to lead him into a passionate activism at one time and into severe depression at other times. They also fear that John will choose to go to jail or flee to Canada rather than be drafted.

Steve, two years younger than John, is now nineteen and has been a great problem for Barbara and Allen for some time. He managed to graduate from high school where, though bright, he did little work and took little interest in any of the regular activities. Mostly Steve's interests have been in playing electric guitar in a rock group, motorcycles, and, recently, drugs. Last year Steve was picked up in another state for possession of marijuana along with two other boys with whom he was hitchhiking across the country. Allen flew to his son's side, arranged bail, and hired a lawyer who managed to get the case dismissed on the grounds of illegal search. During that time Allen had to take time off from the office, make two additional trips with Steve out of state for court hearings, and pay the attorney more than a thousand dollars in fees. Steve, though grateful to his father, has seemed to take the help for granted. He has indicated he will repay the money but that he refuses to work at a job he doesn't like in order to do so. At present Steve is living with a girl in a kind of commune and his parents believe he has turned on to other drugs. Their repeated attempts to bring him home and to get him psychiatric counseling have been unsuccessful. Steve frequently contacts his parents for money, which they give him, fearing that if they refuse he may be driven to steal.

Sally, the youngest at sixteen, is both a mystery and a joy

to Barbara and Allen. In appearance Sally is thin and fragile, so that her parents are always bugging her to eat more. Her interest in transcendental meditation, yoga, and health food, as well as her participation in various sensitivity groups, is a far cry from anything they ever experienced in their own youth. However, Sally is a very sensitive girl and aspires to write poetry, for which she shows considerable aptitude. Barbara and Allen are hopeful they can enroll her in a private school for her senior year in high school in order to prepare her for college as well as to lessen the kind of bad influence they feel led Steve astray. Such a school will be very expensive, but they feel it would be worth it.

But not only are Barbara and Allen trying to cope with the problems of their children, they are also dealing with problems relating to their parents. When Allen's father died three years ago, his mother, then seventy-five, insisted on continuing to live in the same house alone. It soon became clear that she was not able to manage such an existence; so when she refused to even consider a rest home she came to live with Barbara and Allen. There were a great many tensions for a while, especially between Allen's mother and the two grandsons, John and Steve. Barbara felt continually pulled between the two generations, coming close to having a mental breakdown the previous year when Steve was arrested and Allen's mother blamed her for being too permissive. Now Allen's mother remains secluded most of the time in her room, refusing to come out for anyone but her son. Meals are taken to her on a tray.

Barbara's parents—her father is sixty-eight and her mother sixty-five—have always been very independent and gregarious, living in a modest apartment after they sold their family home because it was too big for them. They were able to manage financially on their social security and some money they had saved. Recently, however, Barbara's mother suffered a mild stroke and was in the hospital for two months receiving physical therapy. During that time Barbara spent two weeks with her father, then hired a housekeeper to give him assistance. Her mother has now recovered enough to come home. Barbara and Allen have spent long hours looking for a rest home for her parents but have found only two that seemed to them to have any warmth and life to them at all. Most were what they came to describe as "plastic fantastic" or were much too expensive. Neither of the two homes they would consider have vacancies, but they have placed their names on the waiting list. Her parents would very much like to live in a retirement community nearby where many of their friends are, but it is very expensive. Barbara's brother and sister, both across the country with families and with less income than Barbara and Allen, have agreed to contribute what they can, but most of the financial load will fall on Barbara's and Allen's shoulders. They have decided to keep the housekeeper and to try to swing the money to move Barbara's parents into the retirement community.

Barbara and Allen have felt desperate for some time but do not know where to turn for help. They have little opportunity to be alone together for any length of time and have started to feel a real strain between them, even in their most intimate moments. Barbara feels guilty about asking her husband to help with her parents when she herself does not work and makes no financial contribution to their household. She has held back telling him this, however, bitterly reasoning to herself that he owes it to her because of what she has had to do for *his* mother.

Allen, in the meantime, is carrying a huge weight of anxiety because he has learned via the grapevine that his job is in danger. Although he was something of a sensation in 1968, increasing the net asset value of his portfolio by 45 percent, the bear market years of 1969 and 1970 have turned him from hero to goat. The widespread national recession and the major losses within the corporation have meant a drastic cutback in personnel, and his highly prized, $65,000-

per-year job has suddenly become one of the expendable ones. Rumors flying in the financial community that money managers highly respected by Allen are facing the corporate axe have intensified his anxiety. He desperately wonders how he will fulfill all his commitments if he loses his job. On the eve of his fiftieth birthday, when he should be on easy street and coasting into the last third of his life, Allen feels he may be at the end of the line. He has tried to tell Barbara but is unable to for fear she will think him a failure. For the first time in his life Allen has started to stay at his club drinking in the evening after telling Barbara he has to work late.

The case of Barbara and Allen is not atypical, even though they have had to shoulder more than their share of trouble, for this kind of situation is confronting more and more middle-agers. Barbara and Allen feel they hardly exist at all as persons themselves, but are only indispensable guides and guardians in a world they no longer understand, a world that has passed them by. Yet they feel caught in a double bind between the demands of the young and the needs of the old.

REVIEWING THE BALANCE SHEET

When Babe Ruth retired from baseball with his staggering record of 714 home runs, he reputedly was asked if he had any regrets about his career, to which he retorted, "Sure, I wish I'd hit 715 homers." [4] Perhaps human nature is such that a person is incapable of ever being satisfied with his achievements. Whatever its source, this dissatisfaction with the record of one's life looms with terrifying force as a leading symptom of the middlescent malaise.

The depressingly popular game which forty- and fifty-year-olds play with deadly seriousness has been called "Bal-

[4] Quoted by Stanley Frank, *The Sexually Active Man Past Forty* (New York: The Macmillan Company, 1968) , p. 108.

ance Sheet" by the late Eric Berne, author of *Games People Play*. Upon arriving at middle age, each person, in his own way, begins an agonizing reappraisal of his life, his achievements versus his goals, his satisfactions versus his values. While such a review is a meaningful and weighty matter, it is at best subjective and speculative. Our recollections are often distorted, events and feelings only partly remembered. The poet-author John Updike describes a lifelong past as "after all but a vast sheet of darkness in which a few moments, pricked apparently at random, shine." Nevertheless, the stocktaking takes place with a fierce, sometimes life-and-death determination, for somewhere in the summary the person hopes to discover a self-authentification, a self-identity, an assurance that life has been worth the struggle and that he is somebody because of it.

Thus the game of Balance Sheet may dissolve into a real identity crisis, a period in which the middle-ager tries desperately to unscramble his sense of his own selfhood and perhaps reintegrate his personality around a new, more reasonable sense of identity. Who am I? Why did I do what I did? Is this all there is to life? Where do I go from here? These and similar questions grow out of the malaise. Whether a person has been primarily a pessimist or an optimist about life, this period of searching during middlescence tends to accentuate the negative. When one seems mired in the slough of despondency, whether the facts warrant such feelings of despair, it is awfully hard to see the daylight at the end of the tunnel.

Part of the identity crisis means facing the fact that certain choices in the past may have robbed the person of present options in middle age. One such person, interviewed by Barbara Fried for a study on the middle-age crisis expressed his torment and unhappy sense of betrayal like this:

> Sure, I feel trapped. Why shouldn't I? Twenty-five years
> ago a dopey eighteen-year-old college kid made up *his*

mind that *I* was going to be a dentist. So now here I am, a dentist. I'm stuck. What I want to know is, who told that kid he could decide what I was going to have to do for the rest of my life? [5]

Whereas in our youth we are filled with awareness of infinite possibilities and unlimited horizons, in our forties or fifties we must live with what we have actually become. No longer is it possible to say "I'll show them!"—we've had twenty years to do that. The moment of truth has arrived and its recognition is ofttimes shocking. No longer can we kid ourselves that if we don't make it in one line of work we can always try something else. Even in our thirties we could blame luck and fate, and could feel some confidence that relentless effort and determination would help realize our dreams. Now we must acknowledge that we have pretty much done what we are capable of doing. The person in the throes of the middlescent malaise becomes painfully aware that what he thinks of himself is much more important than the opinion of others.

For many, the review of the balance sheet brings a deep sense of "destination failure." In a rare moment of honesty the truth surfaces: the goal set earlier in life is still remote and probably will never be attained. Willie Loman, the tragic anti-hero of Arthur Miller's classic play *Death of a Salesman* expresses the longing of all of us when he says "A man can't go out just the way he came in. He's got to amount to something." Willie Loman is one of the many who identified "amounting to something" with being successful in business and he couldn't make it. And certainly the Willie Lomans are to be found in various professions—education, law, medicine, the clergy, as well as door to door salesman.

In a study of the middle-aged male it was discovered that the period of self-appraisal begins in dead earnest around

[5] Barbara Fried, *The Middle-Age Crisis* (New York: Harper & Row, 1967) , p. 59.

the age of forty-three, leading the person to test and examine his career to see whether it has worked out the way he planned. He may arrive at one of four conclusions:

1. *He is a failure.* In this case the man may try to escape his own conclusion through alcoholism, suicide, or a protective stoicism which accepts the fact that "that is just the way it is." The "grandiose failure" or the "embittered genius" rationalizes that he is too good, too fine, or too far ahead of his time to be appreciated as a way to account for his failure.

2. *The results are inconclusive.* This, the study points out, is the most common adjustment men make, and enables the person to keep on in the hope that something will turn up yet.

3. *He has been partially successful.* This conclusion provides the person with the best chance of happiness, giving him a sense of fulfillment while helping him modify goals that were too high.

4. *He has been successful.* The interesting thing here is that while ideally the person who arrives at this conclusion should be happiest, such is rarely the case. Rather, the man tends to feel dissatisfied with the goals he chose or with the road he took that brought him where he is.

In terms of this last point, then, we may ask whether Willie Loman, were he a highly successful salesman, would have been able to say on his balance sheet, "I know who I am, I am somebody. I am happy." The answer is, "not necessarily," because, oddly enough, many people who are most successful in the eyes of the community are most deeply afflicted by fear of their own failure when they hit the middlescent malaise.

Consider a man in a midwestern community whom we shall call Tom Smith. He is president of a corporation at forty years of age, has a beautiful wife, owns an estate with tennis courts and swimming pool, is very prominent in the community—chairman of the United Crusade and the Republican party in the county, and so on. One day a friend said to him, "Tom, you must be living on top of the world. You have everything going for you, a wonderful family, a lovely home, a beautiful wife, a successful business, community recognition." Tom replied, in effect, with some difficulty, "But if you only knew! I have this deep sense of failure for some reason I can't even explain. Look at me, just look at me! I'm a graduate of Harvard Business School with an M.B.A. I'm a Rotarian, an Episcopalian, a Republican. I belong to the Country Club. I'm a first class WASP. I feel like a programmed robot." What Tom is feeling is that he is no longer the maker and master of his own life, that he merely fills niches, Republican, Rotarian, corporation president, Episcopalian, Harvard graduate, all the rest. His success does not alleviate his feeling of being trapped—of being a captive of his own social status. Tom's balance sheet reveals his sense of the "failure of success."

One of the lessons taught by the balance sheet game is that achievements themselves cannot bring personal fulfillment to anyone. They can be rewarding for those who already have a sense of their own worth and adequacy as persons, but the satisfaction of feeling at home in one's body as it is, of knowing where one is in the world, requires a sense of identity that comes from within.

Along with the fear of failure in work, the middle-ager often feels a sense of failure in relation to family life. If, during that tender period, the man's wife continues to count on him for achieving all the great things he was going to do, he sees her as too demanding, but if she drops her unrealistic expectations, he accuses her of no longer believing in him. Or he may suddenly decide to give his children the attention he always wanted to give them, only to find that they have their own friends and peer-group interests and are virtual strangers. Imagine his shock when his twelve-year-old daughter blurts out, "I hate you, Dad." Had he stayed home with the family before, he reasons, he might not have gotten the promotions and raises, but now all they seem to want from him is money. Furthermore, when his son goes to work he may make more money on his first job than his father earned after ten years of struggles. What frustration! One father said to his son with a trace of bitterness, "Why do you think you're entitled to find work that makes you happy? I made it by the rules of the game, why can't you? I worked all my life in a mundane, routine job that I simply endured in order to give the family security." In this case the balance sheet gets marked under the heading "feel cheated."

During the middlescent malaise the fear of death may loom as one of the most painful and frantic sources of apprehension, with one's personal death regarded somehow as a kind of ultimate proof of failure. Partly, of course, the middle-ager is brought close to the reality of death through experiences with parents and older friends. But in the balance sheet game, the face of death provides a clear boundary line for the evaluation. Time is running out, the moments of life are ticking away, even now it is too late to make up for the debit side—the unanswered calls, the wasted opportunities, the neglected values, the unreceived gifts, the guilt. The person who has always slept soundly may find himself in middle age a restless sleeper or a dreamer of nightmares, who suddenly wakes up in the wee, small hours of the morning in a state of inexplicable anxiety and panic. T. S. Eliot has aptly described this phenomenon as the age of the hoo-ha's:

> When you're alone in the middle of the night and you
> Wake in a sweat and a hell of a fright
> When you're alone in the middle of the bed and you
> Wake like someone hit you in the head
> You've had a cream of a nightmare dream and you've
> Got the hoo-ha's coming to you.[6]

[6] T. S. Eliot, "Fragment of an Agon," from *Sweeney Agonistes* in *Complete Poems and Plays*, p. 84. Used by permission of Harcourt Brace Jovanovich and Faber & Faber.

If the person feels some sense of integrity, some awareness of his own self as a unique personality with experiences only he could have, then he may be able to view his death as a part of the process inherent in the life cycle itself. But the person who has lost his self-esteem and has a sense of failure may experience deep despair.

Consideration of physical health comes in for close scrutiny in the middlescent game of balance sheet, and there is often undue preoccupation with the body. Changes in appearance could be accepted in stride in the thirties, but by forty-five the cumulative effects of the aging process can no longer be ignored. Stocktaking in this area may lead to general irritability and incredulity, or to severe depression and anxiety. There may be a sudden surge of fatigue, accompanied by poor sleep, both manifestations of internal rebellions and conflicts.

Viewing herself in the mirror day after day, the middle-aged woman may give up and just let herself go, telling herself it doesn't matter anyway if she's overweight and behind the times in fashion—"Who can keep up with changing hair styles and hem lengths anyway?" Or she may go to the other extreme and spend half her time in a beauty parlor or a small fortune on creams and lotions, exercisers, facial suanas, hair tints, diet pills, and a new wardrobe for each of her possible sizes, depending on how successful she is at trimming her figure.

The middle-aged man usually reacts to health concerns in one of two ways, sometimes switching from one to the other. He may become overcautious, hoping to stay young by keeping his body fit. In this case he diets to extreme, lies under the sun lamp (at least he'll *look* healthier!), starts jogging and exercising, and periodically gives up smoking and drinking—or he may throw caution to the winds and set out to prove to himself and others that he is still a fit physical specimen by competing vigorously with the younger men.

The person adapting in this manner laughs at diets and exercises, drinks and smokes as much as ever—and usually shortens his life about ten years in the process.

Results from reviewing the balance sheet vary, of course, and the person who brings into middle age a sense of his own validity and worth can weather his own scathing self-judgment. But too often the middle-ager discovers a real dislike of himself and gravely doubts his ability to cope with his own fears and responsibilities. Such a person, in his anxiety about the future and his guilt over the past, is unable to live in a real present. He cannot face his "now" like it is and continue to live with himself, so he takes refuge in a make-believe life that is more comfortable.

> So we play a game with time, pretending a glorious past and a promising future, but no present. Although it is a fantasy, we take the game with a certain absurd seriousness. In our romanticisms we dream of those good old days, and in our messianisms we dream of the great deliverances to come; but in the meantime we live as if the present had no being, or as if its being had no value. Real values and means lie behind us and before us in time, but certainly not now.[7]

Middle age—the nonsense time, the in-between time, the worst time of your life—if you are afflicted with the middlescent malaise.

Reviewing the balance sheet is an ongoing process to which the middlescent malaise gives exaggerated importance. When we overemphasize the past and future, a curious thing happens in relation to the present: in the midst of our anxiety, insecurity, and negation, we are bored with the "now"! Let us move to a consideration of this new symptom.

[7] Thomas C. Oden, *The Structure of Awareness* (Nashville: Abingdon Press, 1969), p. 188.

BORE, BORING, BORED

Helen Brown made an appointment with her minister. She arrived very depressed, having obviously been crying, and though only thirty-nine she had the appearance more like a woman of fifty, poorly groomed, unattractively dressed. Helen had made a decision to divorce Harry, her husband of eighteen years, on the following grounds: he was an unfaithful husband, an excessive drinker, a neglectful father, and a poor provider. In spite of these "valid reasons" for divorce, however, she tearfully acknowledged she still loved Harry and did not really want to go through with it. The minister suggested that both of them come to talk before making a final decision.

When Helen and Harry arrived, a couple of weeks later, she appeared in much the same state, though a little more hostile and judgmental. Harry seemed amazingly uninvolved emotionally in his manner, remaining relaxed and almost "far away" throughout the interview as his wife unleashed her verbal bombardment against him. He admitted having relations with other women all his life, indicating it had been that way with his father and it was that way with him. His drinking was perhaps a little heavy, he supposed, but not a problem. He said his business would be successful if given a little time (though a few days later the courts padlocked the doors and he later filed for bankruptcy). Harry generally appeared unfeeling, unaware of his wife's pain and unable to see why she was so upset. After all, he said, things were not much different from the way they had been with them for seventeen years!

Harry's last observation was precisely true, of course: Life in their marriage had not changed much in seventeen years. There had been little sharing of deep feelings, almost no personal growth on the part of either husband or wife, and, if their marriage had ever had any romance or excitement, it had fled long ago. The only "change" had been Helen's increasing consciousness that she felt trapped in a meaning-less relationship and had to do something about it.

If Helen or Harry, or any number of couples suffering from the same impasse, were to be asked how they honestly felt about their marriages, the response would no doubt sound like Leo Herman, a character in Herb Gardner's play *A Thousand Clowns.* Leo's former scriptwriter Murray Burns asks him how his TV show ("Chuckles the Chipmonk") is going, and Leo answers with vehemence, ". . . boring, boredom, bore, "then cupping his hands around his mouth he continues to shout, "boring, boring, boring—." Trapped into playing roles that are childish and immature, the hus-band and wife perpetuate a marriage that over the years becomes more like a farce, or a dumb show, than a real-life drama in which people grow and change.

In this case Helen and Harry made no progress in their counseling, and finally Helen initiated divorce proceedings. Within six months Harry was married to a new spouse. Helen began to show a little more spark in her life, was more careful in her appearance, and started taking an active part in community activities.

This marriage is only one of many that give validity to the conclusion that boredom (from the root word *bore,* meaning "to make something empty") and overindulgence in alcohol to relieve the boredom are among the chief causes of middle-age divorces. Boredom has been called the endemic disease of captive audiences, observable in caged animals in zoos, for instance, who avoid their ennui by sleeping. Seen in this perspective, boredom is one of the basic problems facing mankind today. H. L. Mencken once observed that "the capacity of human beings to bore each other seems to be vastly greater than that of any other animal's."

Samuel Beckett's now classic play *Waiting for Godot* is one of the most profound and powerful experiences of man's sense of emptiness and boredom that has ever been expressed. In this drama the two central characters, Vladimir (Didi) and Estragon (Gogo), are captives in two senses: individually, each is a captive audience to the other in their mutual dependence; together, they are a captive audience to time in their hope that their waiting will be fulfilled. As they wait the two of them go through all the antics that men everywhere have used to cope with their boredom: they attend to their bodily needs, they discuss, speculate, contradict each other, abuse each other, fight, and then make up. But when each game is over the boredom is still there. At one point Didi speaks aloud his inner thoughts: "We have time to grow old. The air is full of our cries. But habit is a great deadener." [8]

This observation brings us back to the warning made by Balzac: "Marriage must continually conquer the monster that devours, the monster of habit." When two people hold each other captive in marriage, with one or both partners dissatisfied with the stimuli proffered and wanting something else (and probably not even knowing what the something else might be), boredom becomes public enemy number one. Habit, routine, sameness, emptiness, disenchantment, the feeling of being taken for granted, a blah feeling, a lack of any sense of value—all these are variations on the same theme.

> We cease to notice or to be pleased by the painting that has hung on our wall for a decade; we grow accustomed and dulled to the love we won long ago. The face that was endlessly absorbing, the touch that was electrifying, the personality that was fascinating, eventually become merely comfortable, like the morning's scrambled eggs and coffee. For a while this may seem tolerable, but as the years dwindle in which one might yet recapture the lost intensity, a certain desperation appears.[9]

[8] Samuel Beckett, *Waiting for Godot* (New York: Grove Press, 1954), pp. 58-59.
[9] Hunt, *The Affair*, p .36.

There was a time when people did not live as long, worked harder simply to secure the necessities of food, shelter, and clothing, and did not expect as much from life. Marriage meant companionship, progeny, labor, and eventual death. But today we can and do expect more than humdrum weariness.

A good part of our problem is our inablity to hang on to excitement in the familiar or to interject novelty into the routine. Thus we often invite boredom into our marital relationship by simply neglecting the partner and his growth as a person. On the one side, there is the neglected husband. If his wife works they obviously must make some kind of mutual adjustment, but perhaps she is just not aware of his needs—the importance of a clean shirt for the business conference, a good meal at the end of a hard day. Perhaps she and the children, together more than he is with either of them, begin to leave him out of conversations and family planning. He may go along for quite a while because he does not want to cause trouble, but after so long he becomes bored. Or maybe his wife, caught up in the frantic round of community activities, is so busy doing good in the neighborhood and the church that husband and family get only the leftover enthusiasm and energy.

But there is also the neglected wife. A case was reported in the English-speaking newspaper in Japan of a busy executive's wife who was found beaten, bound, gagged, and raped four times—not once but four times. Several days later the same newspaper carried the story that it didn't happen four times, it only happened three times. She had exaggerated and embellished the story. A few days later the newspaper reported that the police did some more investigation and discovered it did not happen three times, it only happened twice. You can probably guess the inevitable. Upon further inquiry it turned out the incident never took place at all. It was purely a figment of her own imagination. She gagged and beat and lacerated herself to make it appear as if she had been attacked. The obvious question was "why?" Why did this lovely wife of a busy, high-echelon executive do this? Her answer was "I am a neglected housewife." She said that her husband was either always working or out being entertained or playing golf and that she never saw him. She felt neglected and referred to herself as a "golf widow." In order to get any attention from her husband she had to dramatize her plight. She got bored always being alone.

So the neglect can come from either or both sides in the form of too much outside activity by one or the other partner. While the golf widow, as in the case above, is a familiar figure, so also is the bridge widower. In themselves these activities seem harmless enough, even healthy opportunities to be with one's own friends, but, when carried to extreme as rigid necessities, they cause trouble.

> The deadly thing for a marriage is the grooves: *every* afternoon at bridge, *every* Saturday at the golf course. Every marriage needs some privacy, some room for special interests, some breathing spaces. But the end of it is to come together again richer than before. Once the grooves are hardened the marriage tends to run in them.[10]

The grooves become ruts, and a rut, as someone once quipped, is a grave with both ends gone.

On the other hand, the couple that never does anything is in for problems too. Newlyweds begin their marriages with a high amount of leisure time spent together, a continuation of the kind of dating that brought them together in the first place. Then over the course of years this pattern declines, even though the partners continue to have the same preference for what they like to do. Remember the old, bad joke about a husband and wife who were sitting in their kitchen enjoying a cup of coffee when they heard a terrific explosion coming from the house next to them? Rushing to the window,

[10] Rodenmayer, *I John Take Thee Mary*, p. 131.

they saw their neighbors come flying out the window from the force of the explosion, and the man turned to his wife and said, "That's the first time those two have been out together since they were married." If it is always too much trouble to get ready, or one or the other is always too tired, the couple gets out of the habit of going out together. But "getting out of the habit" leads to a new habit which is deadly. When there is simply the same routine each evening, the same television programs, when there are no outside contacts to bring new interest and pleasure into the life of the marriage, the stage is set for the vague restlessness, emptiness, dullness, sameness that spells "boredom."

The decrease in shared activities is often accompanied by a decline in verbal exchange as well. In the early days of the marriage the husband wanted to report everything about his day at the office to his wife. As he did so, her knowledge increased and he began to feel that everything he said resembled what he had already told her, so he gradually stopped talking very much, except to complain about rising costs and the commuter traffic. Similarly, the wife used to tell her husband everything that happened in her day, at home, shopping, with the baby, until she lost interest in the repetition. Her conversation deteriorated into a chronicle of the day's woes. Add to this declining exchange of any deep personal meaning the rising pattern of suppressing real feelings and reactions which might lead to conflict, and you get, once more, the stagnant pool which breeds boredom.

A couple, whose boredom led them to consider divorce, were counseled to express their real reactions in an effort to break their encrusted habit of avoiding conflict. The writer describes what happened: "On the very first occasion when the woman brought out her negative reaction to some unconsciously selfish act on the part of her husband, he sat up and looked at her with a new attention, saying, 'Why, you're interesting when you talk like that!' " [11] Both partners

[11] Harding, *The Way of All Women*, p. 167.

realized their mistake in fearing they would lose the other's affection if they were honest. Some such kind of radical breakthrough is needed to dispel the boredom of the middlescent malaise.

Boredom is not, as many of us suppose, only the absence of excitement; it is far more insidious and treacherous than that. At first we accept the fact that marriage must lose its first bloom and routine must become the norm. By the time we arrive at middlescence the problem has already taken its toll—in hardened ruts, erratic behavior, loss of feeling and sensitivity. It is typical for the bored person to suffer in silence. But the hidden malady can be detected in the exaggerated and frantic search for something fun and pleasurable, or in the restless inability to concentrate on work or family, or in the shifts in mood from lethargic puttering to intense fury or hypertension.

The American housewife who finds her talents frustrated or her desires for self-fulfillment blocked is especially susceptible to what a psychiatrist has called the "four B's syndrome": Bridge, Bourbon, Bonbons, and Boredom. And the greatest of these, of course, which aggravates the rest by gnawing at her soul, is boredom.

The *New York Times* recently reported the case of a housewife who tried to fight boredom by working alongside her husband in a mineshaft a hundred feet underground. When asked why she did such difficult and dirty work way down in the mineshaft, she replied: "Just to get away from the boredom of being around the house." There are many women who cannot find meaning for themselves in the monotony and drudgery of routine housework and who seek a fulfillment all their own. For some it results in more and more perilous pastimes: the suburban key party, the bottle, or the casual love affair. Many housewives yearn for the constant stimuli that their husbands experience in the workaday world. Their husbands meet new and interesting and exciting persons as well as situations.

Boredom, once recognized, can provide a special opportunity for renewal and discovery—of oneself, of one's spouse, of what we value, of what gives meaning to our existence. In the experience of being bored—of being made empty—the real question is, What is absent that would give me or us meaning and fulfillment? Human beings are really much too complex and complicated to become boring. One doctor suggests that "people never become boring unless one stops looking at them and listening to them; or if one was only using them in the first place." [12]

Boredom is one of the chief symptoms of the middlescent malaise. A bored person is one whose life has been made empty, a vacuum. But the story does not end here. Nature abhors a vacuum and something will be found sooner or later to fill the void.

TRAUMA OF LOST YOUTH

A fourth symptom of the middlescent malaise is the sense of loss that comes when we realize our youth is indeed gone forever, and with it our illusion of omnipotence and immortality. There is a desperate longing for the carefree days when we seemed free to do and be whatever we wanted, for now we yearn for change but find habit and routine too difficult to break. We also find ourselves less employable and more expendable; we experience ourselves as less physically attractive and therefore less desirable. Whereas once we smiled with recognition at seeing two young people embracing, we now suddenly become depressed, envious, nostalgic, and painfully aware that if we behave in like manner we are called lecherous dirty-old-men.

Our initial reaction to finding ourselves on the downhill side of life is usually shock, from which we pass into a stage that psychiatrists have called "emotional second adolescence."

[12] Robert B. McCready, *Our Bed Is Flourishing* (New York: Sheed and Ward, 1969), p. 120.

Here a middle-age revolt is launched against time, fate, and circumstances, a defiant and somewhat violent attempt to postpone the inevitable aging by recapturing the exciting pursuits of youth. As we might expect, such reassertion of adolescent desires usually includes an emphasis on sexual behavior, a kind of advanced repetition of the fears and reassurances experienced at puberty. Thus the wife finds herself feeling vibrantly alive and titillated with excitement in the presence of a delightful, charming gentleman who showers her with attention at a dinner party; the husband gets turned-on in a way he hasn't known for years as he chats at a cocktail party with a dark, beautiful stranger. Of course the wife doesn't have to see her elegant stranger in his pajama bottoms in the morning or listen to him grind his teeth. And the husband has not had to look at his lady beautiful in hair curlers or with a migraine headache. Both have fallen back into the notion of romantic love where such mundane considerations are swept aside.

In pursuit of lost youth the middle-ager falls victim to his old illusions and phantasies, seeing in the stranger the ideal image of the one he or she should have married and with whom the present predicament obviously would never have happened. Perhaps there is only idle daydreaming about an actual extramarital affair, but the more one fantasizes, the more the barriers to such an event are lowered. At this point, when the marriage may be at its most rocky stage anyway in terms of intimacy between the partners, it may be easy for one or the other (or both) to rationalize that a person has a right to get a little happiness out of life before it's too late, and so succumb to an adventurous amorous encounter.

Though the classic love story makes the fascinating stranger (who can set the body chemistry surging again in its quest to relate to some other person) the eventual partner in the affair, it is usually true that first affairs almost always involve friends already known and close at hand. Here, of course, propinquity plays a major part, but somehow the lovers are convinced they have been thrust into the grip of passion by some special kind of fate.

Affairs of rebellion usually involve poor judgment on the part of the people who choose each other. Because the youthful, unabashed self is in operation, the ardent one almost always chooses someone with whom a truly satisfying relationship is impossible. This may also stem from an unconscious guilt about the infidelity. People who feel guilty want to be punished, and how better to ensure punishment than to choose someone who will provide frustration and suffering?

One doctor suggests that most middle-age rebellions among men are not, deep down inside, really intended to be serious. The man protests his own aging biological makeup, believing that if he could return to his first adolescence his new knowledge and maturity would prevent his making the same mistakes. Standing in the way in his own mind, however, is his wife. The rebel's conscious thoughts run like this:

> I want happiness, love, approval, admiration, sex, youth. All this is denied me in this stale marriage to an elderly, sickly, complaining, nagging wife. Let's get rid of her, start life all over again with another woman. Sure, I'll provide for my first wife and my children; sure, I'm sorry that the first marriage didn't work out. But self-defense comes first; I just *have* to save myself! [13]

Underneath, the rebel is saying he is a washout, a failure, and unless he gets happiness in a hurry he will not be able to stand his own psychic punishment. But though the husband may not really intend to carry through with divorce, the wife may refuse to take him back from an affair and out he goes. If she handles the situation right, he usually returns to her and his home with good nature, resigned and tired, and more accepting of the inevitable.

[13] Edmund Bergler, *The Revolt of the Middle-Aged Man* (New York: Grosset and Dunlap, 1954), pp. 75-76.

A case which was not so smoothly resolved, however, is the marriage of Irene and Dan. Married for fifteen years, they have a family of three children, whose ages are twelve, nine, and eight. Dan has enjoyed a reasonably successful career as a newspaper reporter and photographer. His human interest pictures have occasionally appeared in national magazines, giving him a flash of local notoriety. A devout and impeccably neat person, Irene has been content to maintain a good home and family life, and enjoys being "just a housewife" who takes seriously her responsibility of being a good mother.

Irene had thought the marriage was coasting along pretty well after a major squabble over finances was resolved some five years ago. Suddenly Dan began returning home late at nights. At first Irene thought her husband was on special assignment for the newspaper and was growing a beard for the task. When Dan stayed away from home for two nights, Irene sensed that all was not well. Her feelings alternated between fear and anger. She called the newspaper and the police but got no helpful leads.

After Dan returned and Irene asked his whereabouts, Dan replied casually and coolly that he was just "out doing my thing," and that he had quit his job and was dropping out. During the heated exchange of words that followed, Dan accused Irene of being hung-up on straight, superficial, middle-class values of materialism and respectability; whereas Irene charged that Dan was irresponsible, lazy, ruining his life and career, and turning into a long-haired bum who would soon be after a handout from the welfare department. Dan took a sleeping bag from the closet, and with a smile on his lips waved goody-bye.

Days later, on a shopping trip, Irene was driving through a sector of town known as a hangout for hippies when suddenly she spotted Dan in front of a psychedelic music shop. His arm was wrapped around a skinny, long-haired girl dressed in tie-dyed clothes, who couldn't have been a day over seventeen. Dan smiled gaily and flashed a peace sign with his free hand at Irene as she drove by in a state of shocked stupor and disbelief.

That is the last time Irene ever saw Dan. He didn't even bother to pack his belongings. He simply left the house and children and moved into a commune with his young hippie friends. A stunned Irene could give no explanation for her thirty-eight-year-old husband's relapse into second adolescence. She was left wondering why Dan can't "act his age and stop being so childish." Finally she initiated divorce proceedings, took a secretarial job, and set out to raise the children herself.

The phenomenon of the middle-aged man's rebellion— what Dr. Bergler calls "the measles of the late forties and early fifties"—represents such a repetitious pattern that someone once remarked: "All husbands are alike, but they have different faces so you can tell them apart." [14]

A flight to the sensation of sex for the middle-ager may give some temporary comfort to him in his middlescent malaise. Perhaps he rediscovers himself as a lover. A man who was unable to speak romantic words suddenly finds himself a poet as he relates to this new love. A woman who felt incapable of certain sexual acts with her husband finds them now fascinating and wholesome. Morton Hunt, in his study for *The Affair,* discovered that one-third of his respondents admitted a feeling of pride about their first affair, and a majority indicated they felt happier, younger, and more self-confident "at least part of the time." Why, we might ask, could these same people not discover these new dimensions of themselves with their spouses? To such a question the answer would probably be "he wouldn't understand," or "nothing new could ever happen with her," and so on.

But while the extramarital affair is sometimes the soothing remedy for the trauma of lost youth, the sexual relationship alone does not bring healing to the spirit of middle-agers.

[14] *Ibid.,* p. 6.

Their conquests of the other sex bring temporary challenge and excitement, but the lovers seldom give themselves time to know each other; indeed they often avoid deep intimacy, as though allowing such a thing would break the spell. The middle-age rebel is often an enigma to himself, as is discernible in the following comment one man made concerning his continued affairs:

> What do I get out of it? Not what I got with Jennifer, not at all. So why do I do it? To make myself feel young, I suppose. To get away with something. Maybe just to relieve boredom. I don't know. . . . But if my wife is so marvelous, why isn't she enough for me? I wish I knew. She loves me and I love her, and it's very nice, very comforting. But it leaves me feeling middle-aged and settled, and I'm not willing to accept that. Yet I don't want anything like the Jennifer business again, so I run after women I don't care about. I play the game, I chase them, I get laid, I go home feeling good for a little while. . . . But the truth is, I'm not as happy as a man should be who has everything I have. Go figure it out.[15]

Perhaps the sexual frontier has become one of the last places where modern males, conditioned for security, can continue to explore with a sense of daring and risk, and as a way to keep testing themselves. When put in this spot, however, sexuality loses the kind of personal dimension necessary to its expression as a creative source of inspiration and vitality. Sex as conquest and ego-building almost inevitably brings frustration and boredom.

There was a time, also, when a person in middle age, faced with the trauma of lost youth, could gain vicarious indentification with the young and could pretend through them that their experiences continued to be his experiences. One example is the way old grads used to return to their Alma Mater, nostalgically look up the old room in the fraternity

[15] Hunt, *The Affair*, p. 270.

house, and imagine the students living there as an extension of himself and his classmates. The current breed of college students and the generation gap itself has pretty much blown that fantasy. Many fraternity houses—once elegant and now delapidated—all over the country are on the financial skids and are closing down for lack of interest. Students won't support them and the alumni enthusiasm flags after efforts to keep group spirit and tradition alive are rebuked, if not ridiculed.

A recent article in the *Saturday Review* examines the dramatic differences between the Class of 1960 and the Class of 1970 at one particular college, noted for its academic excellence. The author, a member of the 1960 "silent generation" class of graduates, concludes that the two groups could not be farther apart. His analysis of the decade between them bears repeating:

> In the intervening ten years, of course, the campus and the world have been remade. The campus has become heavy with causes, the world heavy with woes. The Class of '61 got caught up in the idealism of John F. Kennedy, the Class of '62 became aware of civil rights. Since then, students have had pollution, starvation, and oppression to battle, as well as a war to fight.
>
> What has the Class of '60 been doing while all this has been happening? Sad to say, not much. The Silent Generation has slipped quite comfortably into the Silent Majority, thank you. Instant middle age.[16]

If this is true of the Class of 1960, think of what has happened to the Class of 1950 or 1940, which represents the graduating period for most middle-agers. Poles apart from the present generation of students, those undergoing the trauma of lost youth are in a double bind: they want to go back but there is nothing identifiable in the present to which

___

[16] Mike Gartner, "The Silent Generation Meets the Class of 1970," *Saturday Review* (August 15, 1970), p. 52. Copyright 1970 Saturday Review, Inc.

they can return. "Alumni Day" on many campuses is no longer the occasion for joy and festive celebration. Instead the mood is sad and wistful, a strange and noisy world of protest tinged with pot.

In a widely reprinted article K. Ross Toole, a history professor at the University of Montana, made newspaper headlines when he denounced what he called the new tyranny of the young in favor of a reappraisal of our own middle-class selves and our hard-won progress. The tone of his frustrated outburst is evident in the following sample passage:

> I am tired of being blamed, maimed and contrite; I am tired of tolerance and the reaching out (which is always my function) for understanding. I am sick of the total irrationality of the campus rebel, whose bearded visage, dirty hair, body odor and tactics are childish but brutal, naive but dangerous, and the essence of arrogant tyranny—the tyranny of spoiled brats.
>
> I am terribly disturbed that I may be incubating more of the same. Our household is permissive, our approach to discipline is an apology and a retreat from standards— usually accompanied by a gift in cash of kind.[17]

Caught in the middlescent malaise, with the pressures mounting from all sides, the victim comes out fighting. Now he too looks back in anger. He is indeed squeezed between the needs of the old and the wants of the young who depend on him. He bears the brunt of both generations. Middlescent man is not terribly comfortable standing in the middle—the middle of his career, the middle of his life, the middle of his marriage. He has doubts about whether he has accomplished anything as he critically reviews his lfe. He endures the agony of a good deal of boredom. And his desire to return to his lost youth, when he felt most alive and vital, is spoiled by a current youth subculture that seems so foreign, and, worst yet,

---

[17] *San Francisco Sunday Examiner and Chronicle,* April 5, 1970.

seems to be undermining the values and meaning for which he fought and was willing to defer gratification.

"Facing it like it is" in those areas takes courage—and we're only halfway through the process. Now we move to take a closer look at the impact of this middlescent malaise on the marital relationship, and we discover that the complication created by the onslaught of middle age has now become a full-fledged crisis.

IV

SUSPENSE: SPOTLIGHT ON SEX

As the second act of the marriage drama continues to unfold, we confront complications aggravated by the middlescent malaise. Our spotlight now turns to sex as we look with candor at the sex life of middle-aged couples.

Since the bond of marriage admits its lovers to the basic ritual of intimate sexual love, this aspect of wedded life frequently raises complications and crises of its own. To the extent that a couple's sex life is a kind of barometer for their marriage as a whole, it is appropriate to consider it as the locus for much of the suspense in the marriage drama. "Facing it like it is" always carries with it the suspense of wondering how it will all turn out. And nowhere, perhaps, are there greater attendant feelings of anxiety, frustration, excitement, ecstacy, and anticipation than in the sexual side of marriage during middle age. Sexuality may contribute to the development of the well-made marriage or add misery to the growing spouse gap.

It has been said that "When sexual adjustment in a marriage is good it constitutes about ten percent of the positive part, but when sexual adjustment is bad it constitutes about ninety percent of what is wrong." [1] Said another way, if a couple gets along all right in the bedroom, it is likely they are also getting along fairly well in the rest of the house. But if things are upset in the living room or kitchen or the study or wherever, then it is not surprising to find the bed-

[1] O. Spurgeon English and Gerald H. Pearson, *Emotional Problems of Living,* quoted by Stanley Frank, *The Sexually Active Man Past Forty,* p. 12.

room representing a kind of battlefield where the couple goes to the mat and fights it out. While sexual incompatability can eventually ruin an otherwise good marriage, a satisfactory sexual adjustment by itself cannot make right what may otherwise be wrong in the marriage relationship. And eventually the marital dis-ease will infect the sexual relations as well as the other areas.

If the marriage is out of kilter, then, the sex life of the partners will reflect that lack of zest and spice. Dr. David Reuben, of *Everything You Always Wanted to Know About Sex* fame, has observed that there is a sense in which sex is "optional" in human beings. That is, sex, unlike food and shelter, is not a prerequisite of man's personal survival. The dangers inherent in the middlescent malaise often threaten the marriage in such a way that the couple is reluctant or unable to relate on the sexual level at all. Difficulties of this kind hasten the spouse-gap crisis.

This does not mean that the marriage partners are doomed to a poor sex adjustment. It means that their poor sex life reveals other hostilities and reasons of frustration toward each other. A familiar figure is the wife who complains that her husband expects her to be nice to him in bed on Saturday night after ignoring her all week—"all he wants from me is sex." Thus sexual incompatability can be a cause of marital failure, or a result of it, or an accompanying symptom of the general marital malaise.

The total response relation of two people is motivated ultimately from an all-inclusive emotional state rather than a purely physical one. Sex, as part of that total relationship is the means by which personal feelings of love are expressed. The sex act is a kind of ritual dance, a recurring celebration in which two people participate in an age-old yet renewing pattern of mutual pleasure and satisfaction. There is the immediate pleasure of the excitement and release of tension in orgasm, but there is also the pleasurable consciousness that the couple is participating in the ongoing dance of life

98

in which they celebrate their humanity and their mutual devotion through the ritual of intercourse. From this repetition evolves their own unique, private relationship as a couple in which they build together a common history of memories, shared joys, sensations of pleasure given and received, fulfillment together after times of suffering and struggle, and awareness of the mystery by which their union has brought forth children. A mutually satisfying and responsive experience of sexual intercourse can be one of life's peak moments.

It is true that the very ritual nature of intercourse may lead to boredom for some people. Novelist Mary McCarthy echoes the bored view of sex in *A Charmed Life:* "One screw, more or less, could not make much difference, when she has already laid it on the line for him about five hundred times." For those who find the many subtle adaptations of which human beings are capable in coitus, the very repetition, however, could become the opportunity for discovery and vitality.

For a phase of human activity which is so fraught with possibilities and promises, why then does sex become such a hang-up for both spouses, and so often remain one after many years of marriage?

In order to attack that question we have pinpointed three primary centers where trouble rocks the marriage bed: (1) the chronicle of general sexual ills which plague married life and get intensified with middlescence, Complaint Department; (2) the implications of the "change of life"— the menopause and the climacteric—on both partners, Help Wanted; and (3) the impact of the current changing social mores and views regarding sex and sexuality, Lost and Found.

COMPLAINT DEPARTMENT

There is a story about a couple who had been married for almost twenty years and were experiencing the spouse gap during middlescence. A typical morning at breakfast found the husband and wife deeply engrossed in reading the morning newspaper without any conversation. Suddenly the husband peered over the top of his part of the paper, reached across the table to his unsuspecting wife, and wham! he slapped her across the face, saying, "That's for being such a lousy lover." Then he went back to reading his newspaper. Suddenly from across the table the wife reached out and wham! she slapped her husband across the face and said, "That's for knowing the difference."

When it comes to sex ills and dissatisfactions, this particular couple are but two people in a very long line at the Complaint Department window! How many disgruntled husbands look at their wives and long for a more ravishing bedmate? How many frustrated wives crave for more sensitivity and tender affection?

Probably the basic general answer to the question of sexual complaints rests in the simple fact that any human activity can be used by men and women for destructive as well as for constructive and creative ends. The more delicate and intimate the expression of a relationship, the more likely it is to fall prey to manipulation and misuse. The sex act is the most intimate of all human relationships, with an unspoken language which richly expresses a host of emotional states of being. Through that language we can convey deep love and a desire for total closeness. But we can also convey fear, hatred, and impulse to punish or control, as well as many other such abuses. The very power of the sex drive makes it a viciously effective weapon. Many spouses, therefore, can twist sex to control or punish the partner, perhaps unconsciously but just as completely as if it were planned.

A familiar abuse of sex is the withholding of one's favors in order to gain a material objective or to control a spouse's behavior. Incredible as it sounds, counselors report an endless variation on the example of the wife who won't sleep with her husband until he agrees to let her buy a new dress, or to take her on a vacation, and so forth. Sex is used as tit-for-tat. Or a woman may withhold sex as punishment for things her husband has done that she can't or won't talk about. Consider the case of the couple who went every Sunday to visit the husband's mother. While in his mother's house the man invariably acted like a little boy. When they arrived home and he wanted to make love, the wife shut him off completely because she was so furious. She literally directed so much passion against her mother-in-law that she had none left over for intercourse with her husband.

If the wife uses sex as a weapon primarily by the withholding tactic, the man may use sex to control and retaliate against his wife by insisting on intercourse as his "right" whether she wants to or not. And, of course, the more he insists the more she resists, and the more she resists the more he insists. The "yes-and-no-and-maybe" game can go on *ad infinitum* until one party gets fed up. Suppose the wife flirts at a party, or is late coming home to fix dinner, or is believed to be giving too much attention to the children. The husband may feel threatened by such lack of attention and may regard making his wife submit to him as a way to reestablish his self-esteem. Or, the husband might withhold sex, too, and the couple go for long stretches at a time without intercourse, to see who would give in first.

In such situations the most obvious step toward resolving the sex-centered conflicts would be to confront the matter directly and honestly. Unfortunately, however, sex talk poses one of the primary and most difficult communication blocks in marriage. People married for years may still be embarrassed to talk about sex together (particularly their own sexual relationship) even when it is good. They can have sex and even enjoy it, but they dare not verbalize or acknowledge it. If they find it hard to talk about sex when it is good, how much more difficult for them to discuss their sexual life if there are deep-seated problems! The "discussion" will usually take the form of indignant accusations ("You must be frigid"), or muttered disappointments ("Too tired, I suppose"), or hurt withdrawal ("Another headache?"), or resigned endurance ("Come on, let's get it over with").

A case in point involves a most attractive couple whose marriage finally broke up because they found sex too delicate a matter to discuss. Jerry was a successful engineer and Jane, his wife, taught school. Their childless marriage lasted for thirteen years. The couple engaged in rather perfunctory sexual intercourse about once a month. Jane grew up in a sheltered and strict religious family where her mother, who endured a painful pregnancy and nearly died at Jane's delivery, dinned into her consciousness that sex is dirty and vulgar, an evil to be avoided. As a result she was inhibited and rarely experienced orgasm. At first, Jerry respected her wishes and tried to be sensitive to her sexual revulsion. Three years after their marriage, and faced with mounting pressures of frustration, Jerrry went on a sex binge. He visited a succession of topless bars and four houses of prostitution over the course of a weekend on the pretext of an out-of-town business trip. Not wishing to offend his wife, Jerry still did not feel hc could openly talk about his sexual dissatisfaction with her. Every three years or so, almost following out a cycle, Jerry would become obsessed with sex and go on his big weekend sex binge. Shortly after his last orgy, Jerry decided to divorce Jane, lest he be driven out of his mind. To the end, Jerry's "respect" for Jane was such that he was unable to communicate with her about the sexuality gap that had come between them.

Jerry and Jane's case may be an extreme instance of broken communication, but many couples, in greater or lesser degrees, find it difficult to share their true feelings about sexual intimacy. Generally speaking, a man tends to feel that sexual intercourse can solve misunderstandings and reestablish rapport with his wife, while the woman tends to feel that intercourse is a violation of her if things are not right between them. These adaptations must be talked about

102

in order to be understood and resolved. Sidney Callahan reminds her feminine colleagues that it is possible for the sex act to be an occasion for renewing the broken relationship, instead of a weapon for further punishment: "To suppress sexual desire after a quarrel can be a moral failure—a cold, deliberate refusal to reconcile. The world can 'end in ice, it will suffice,' said Robert Frost. God has given man the fires of desire to warm the world; we flame in his honor as best we can." [2] In any case, to use the sex act as a weapon is a sure way to escalate the spouse-gap crisis.

Two other problem areas which loom large during middle age in regard to coitus concern charges of frigidity or impotence against the partner. Here again discussion could facilitate understanding, but too few couples can be honest enough with each other and with themselves. The wife who feels neglected, who needs more arousal in lovemaking than her husband provides, or who is unable to achieve orgasm is often prematurely judged frigid. And that judgment intensifies her problem and sometimes becomes a self-fulfilling prophecy.

Cautioned for so long to suppress sexual feelings, to discipline herself, to regulate how far she goes with a man in expressing affection, to be careful lest the male take advantage of her, the woman can scarcely become totally free and responsive overnight—literally, over her wedding night. She will need a lot of gentle wooing and loving persuasion to finally get over her past suspicions and let herself enjoy the sensations of genital sexual pleasure. Some women may well need counseling to release the deep, unconscious fears and guilts over sex that were accumulated in childhood, but most need simply a loving context of appreciation and affection within which the sex act is experienced as a natural expression of love between husband and wife.

Listen as a woman, in a study on *The Sexually Responsive*

[2] Sidney Callahan, *Exiled to Eden* (New York: Sheed and Ward, A Search Book, 1969) , p. 151.

Woman by Doctors Phyllis and Eberhard Kronhausen, talks quite openly about her struggle to achieve orgasm in spite of many prior inhibitions. Her personal account runs as follows:

> What, I believe, helped me the most was my husband's understanding attitude, and our mutual feeling that sex was pleasurable and fun. Outside of this, I would say, what proved helpful in liberating me, was that my husband and I informed ourselves as much as possible on sexual matters. By learning more about the facts of sex, we started to become a bit more objective, less emotional—a better word would perhaps be less hysterical about it. That in turn made us sufficiently free to experiment with a wider variety of techniques of love-making to bring more variety into our sex life.
>
> Putting it simply and honestly, I have always learned best by doing.[3]

It is not uncommon for women to say they enjoy intercourse even though they do not experience the complete satisfaction of a climax everytime. But if a husband berates his wife for lack of response in orgasm, she will likely remain permanently unresponsive and may even become truly frigid.

Counselors and psychiatrists note that more and more often these days complaints about lack of sexual satisfaction are coming from wives. Rather than meekly wondering if she is frigid because she doesn't reach orgasm, she says, "My husband does not satisfy me!" Here, again, if there is no discussion of the problem and no attempt to experiment with new ways of lovemaking, the husband may shrink under the criticism of his spouse and become impotent, that is, be unable to perform the sexual act at all by failing to get an erection, by premature ejaculation, or by losing his erection before reaching a climax. Of course, male impotence may also need the help of experienced counselors or therapists if

[3] (New York: Ballantine Books, 1965) , p. 77.

it is deeply rooted in the unconscious layers of past experience. But it is also true that the seeds of male impotence may spring from the relationship itself. For instance, an aggressive woman may unconsciously seek out a passive man to serve her own psychological need to control. She can then belittle him because of his sexual inadequacy and prevent him from being operative at all as a sexual partner.

As the marriage enters its middlescent state, sexual intercourse faces the greatest danger of becoming a ritualistic bore, a cut-and-dried activity, an unexciting and perfunctory habit. This may be particularly true if one or the other partner has never really let go and enjoyed the act. But this is a vicious circle: unless the couple experiments and finds pleasure they will never experience the pleasure discovered by experimenting! The obstacle may be ingrained reluctance to go beyond the direct act of coitus itself or the assumption that there is only one right way, the "missionary position" of man over woman. But enjoyment of intercourse depends largely on the arousal and stimulation of foreplay, especially for the woman. Unless she is an active participant in every phase of the act, neither she nor her husband will ever know what particular sensations please her most. Besides, the husband may get tired of initiating their lovemaking all the time without himself having the experience of having his wife make love to him.

Then, too, people often have preconceived notions about what is "normal" and "abnormal" in sexual relations. More and more counselors are urging couples to regard as normal anything which best meets the physical and emotional needs of the two of them. If their use of sex strengthens, deepens, and intensifies their attachment to each other, it is good. If they alienate and offend and frustrate each other, they need help. But they should remember that they can frustrate each other by not being willing to try new things far more than by doing something different and deciding to discard it as a less desirable technique than others.

Certainly, the first step, even (or perhaps especially) for couples who have known years of bedroom intimacy, is to stop thinking that thoroughly natural impulses are perversions. Social convention has too often arbitrarily dictated what is right and wrong sexual behavior in an attempt to sanctify the pleasure inherent in the act whereby children are conceived while, at the same time, withholding complete approval of the act, on the suspicious grounds that the impulse toward copulation really arises out of man's bestial instincts. But there is increasing recognition that since men and women have been created to copulate, a union which rarely begets children when viewed in terms of its overall frequency, then it is good to take pleasure in sex. A loving couple will share Elizabeth Barrett Browning's sentiment, when she wrote: "How do I love thee? Let me count the ways." Thus any kind of touching, kissing, and stimulation that increases the sensation of pleasure is a desirable area for exploration. For instance, using the mouth to stimulate the sexual organs (called *cunnilingus* when performed on the woman by the man and *fellatio* when performed on the man by the woman) can bring a rise in sensory impulses to a height just short of orgasm itself. In spite of its high erotic response, the general suspicion of genital kissing during foreplay is reflected in the following statistics: "About 60 percent of both the older and younger married people who had been to college engaged in it. There was a sharp drop to 20 percent among couples who had not gone beyond high school and to 11 percent for those whose education stopped after grade school." [4] Young people today tend to take this form of lovemaking for granted, and middle-agers willing to experiment might find it an exciting variation for their own ritual.

Perhaps the response of younger people to oral copulation may be indicated in the experience of a class of college students who attended a seminar on sex which began by showing

[4] Frank, *The Sexually Active Man Past 40*, p. 188.

a series of "skin flicks," explicitly detailing acts of oral love-making. When the lights came on again and the seminar instructor invited feed-back, he was a bit startled by the first student response: "Well, what else is new; we've been doing this since high school."

Not only does the couple need to use a variety of stimuli in the foreplay to intercourse and to vary the repertoire of lovemaking in order to keep the act from being a monotonous and perfunctory performance, but also they need to be open and spontaneous regarding where and when to make love. A couple's sexual relations are almost always governed by the same time and place within the time cycle—the bedroom before going to sleep and in the dark. From a purely practical standpoint, however, the end of the evening is the least favorable time for sex in middle age, since physical energy is at its lowest ebb at that point and the accumulated mental pressures of the day are definitely debilitating to the libido. One writer contends that the chance to copulate at odd hours and in the daylight may be the most intriguing part of an extramarital affair. Making love in the morning, or at lunchtime (note the long "lunch break" enjoyed by Europeans) can bring back lost passion and add zest to the marital relationship.

Having intercourse at a different place can also be invigorating, as indicated in the following wistful account of a man who had been married for years:

But sometimes, when Edwin and Betsy saw a movie or play in which people were deeply in love, he felt vaguely embarrassed that he and she had never had such feelings. Now and then he wanted to seize Betsy and embrace her passionately, but he felt he would look absurd; she would probably laugh, pat him on the cheek, and ask what had come over him. One summer night he wanted to make love in the moonlight on the second-floor porch, but even though no one could have seen them, she said she'd feel self-conscious; besides there might be bugs outside. Yet she almost never refused him sex when he wanted her, and nearly always had orgasm, and for some years Edwin Gottesman thought that his sex life and his marriage were about as good as he could hope for.[5]

Had Edwin and Betsy been able to really talk about their sexual relationship and been open enough to at least try some variations, the good things they had going in their sex life might not have paled over the years. In this particular case Edwin did meet someone else and their marriage broke up.

Too many times couples are hampered by prejudices they hardly know exist. They may even be willing to *do* unconventional things as long as they don't have to recognize or acknowledge them. How much better and direct to discuss the physical expression of love as honestly as any other dimension of the marriage relationship and free it from unspoken prohibitions. By middle age a couple may be too set in a pattern to break out. On the other hand, the very crisis of middlescence itself may bring them to the point where they can experiment, realizing that anything which is a real expression of love may be acceptable to two people. But complaints cannot be attended to unless they are out in the open. The ability of middle-agers to air their sexual difficulties is their best hope of closing the spouse gap.

HELP WANTED

Among the various sex ills that contribute to the middle-age crisis, surely the ones most talked about and analyzed are the menopause for women and the question of a similar change of life for men, usually referred to as the climacteric or the male menopause.

There is, of course, a specified period in a woman's life when her ability to reproduce ceases. Menopause itself means

[5] Hunt, *The Affair*, pp. 39-40.

the end of menstruation, the monthly periods which have kept the woman's womb ready for possible pregnancy during her childbearing years. Since nature arranged things so that women could have their babies while young and strong, the process relating to reproduction changes as they get older. The ovaries secrete less estrogen, gradually stop releasing eggs and cease to function. While we may tend to think of these changes as a single event, they actually take place over a period of time before and after the period we specifically call menopause. The average age for menopause to occur is from 50 to 52, but may well be earlier or later. Certain changes begin as early as age 40, with 40 to 49 called the premenopause period. If a woman has to have both ovaries removed at some point in her reproductive years, there is a reaction called "surgical menopause" which has the same effects as menopause.

Now this biological change sets off a number of real and distressing physical symptoms for the woman, as many of our feminine readers will be quick to attest. First, there are radical variations in menstrual periods, in the amount or duration of flow as well as in the interval between them. The cycles may vary until the woman menstruates perhaps only every two to six months. One of the disturbing things about this aspect of the change, in addition to the annoying inability to be prepared for the periods at a regular time, is the fact that it is still possible to become pregnant during this interval. Since the ovaries still release an egg occasionally there are still times when the woman is fertile. Some women feel a false sense of security during this "dodging" period, thinking they are safe if they have not menstruated in many months, and then end up surprised with a "change-of-life" baby! It is generally felt that a woman should go for at least a full year without any menstrual bleeding before she can stop worrying about becoming pregnant.

Second, the decline in estrogen production produces certain disturbing symptoms including hot flashes and excessive sweating, especially at night. The skin becomes flushed, usually from the shoulders up and the woman feels extremely warm. The frequency of these hot flashes will vary from woman to woman, depending probably on the rate at which the estrogen production ceases. Some women may never experience the disturbance at all because the process takes place so gradually. There are other minor symptoms which include nervousness, irritability, depression, crying spells, headache, dizziness, insomnia, dryness and itchiness along the mucous membranes of the vagina, to cite some of them. Nowadays, if the symptoms are unnecessarily uncomfortable, the doctor can prescribe estrogen therapy as a way to replace the waning hormone supply and provide relief as the biological transition is made in the body. It has been estimated that from 5 percent to 50 percent of female patients require help during the menopause.

For many women the most significant impact of the menopause is psychological. This real, observable change of life objectifies, more than anything else, the fact that she is now middle-aged. If motherhood has been a primary source of self-identity in her life, then the loss of child-bearing ability (even though she did not plan or desire to have more children) may cause a profound depression. There was a time, years ago, when life expectancy was shorter, when a woman was regarded as old when she reached menopause. Now, however, a woman has lived only one-half or two-thirds her expected life span when she undergoes the change from a fertile to an infertile state. A woman is not a "senior citizen" or a useless human being waiting to follow her dying ovaries into oblivion simply because she is going through the change of life.

Too often, of course, the woman looks upon menopause as a personal crisis in identity. However, with medication to help relieve the symptoms and with a more healthy understanding of the process, she may find that the menopause *can* signal a whole new, freeing, rewarding phase of life. For one thing the woman is not bothered by the nuisance of monthly periods and gains a more stable emotional state as her hormone balance levels off from its previous rhythmical cycle. For another thing, she can be freed from the anxiety of pregnancy and can give herself to sexual enjoyment.

Which brings us to the subject of sexual relations at this crisis period. Other than the depression, hot flashes, and other symptoms that may momentarily dampen sexual interest, there is nothing about the menopause which causes a change in sexual feelings, desires, or reponses. The attitude a woman has toward her continuing sex life is a psychologically based one. Here a gradual change in social convention is coming to her aid.

> It has already been said that the male remains capable of producing sperm cells into old age while the female becomes infertile with the onset of the climacteric. This biological distinction used to play an important part in the emotional field as well, for in the former climate of moral opinion sexuality was mainly related to reproduction and recognized as licit only in this respect. Once she could produce no more children, a woman looked upon herself as sexually useless. We now acknowledge that capacity for orgasm has nothing to do with reproduction and that completion of intercourse without desire to reproduce has its own rights; so that sexual consequences of the climacteric have diminished.[6]

Unfortunately, many women in the menopausal or postmenopausal period have been brainwashed to believe that their role as a sex partner and their sexual pleasure diminishes. Therefore, if a woman has never really enjoyed intercourse, she may find this period a convenient excuse to give it up, a regrettable decision almost sure to widen the gap between her and her spouse.

[6] Karl Wrage, *Man and Woman*, trans. Stanley S. B. Gilder (Philadelphia: Fortress Press, 1969) , p. 156.

On the other hand, the woman may find the menopause to be a rejuvenating experience and may actually enjoy sex more than she ever has before. Perhaps she finally finds herself able to cast off her inhibitions and allow her eroticism to grow. With her children gone and a lighter load of household chores, she may find she has more nervous and physical energy for intercourse.

One doctor tells of an older couple who had tapered off to having intercourse every four weeks or so. Then the wife became ill and they had no relations for about six months. When she tried to resume intercourse, the husband could not get an erection. So the wife went out and bought a book on sex, and read that if a wife fondled her husband's penis it helped him have an erection. One might think that this is common knowledge, but she had been taught that playing with sex organs was not something a decent woman did. She bravely tried it anyway and it worked. In fact she experienced their lovemaking as far better than thirty years ago, and her husband as a changed man, cheerful, optimistic, and vigorous. The wife then remarked, "Maybe I shouldn't admit it but I enjoy our relations more than I used to. I'm even thinking of trying some of the other things I read about in that book."

Now certainly this is a case where the potential spouse gap was bridged in a loving, natural, freeing way, where knowledge, not ignorance, was bliss.

Of course, there are situations where the wife may yearn to break the monotony of the conjugal act and be frustrated by her husband's apathy or prudishness. Women are not the only ones influenced by social prejudices! So let us now turn to the phenomenon called the male climacteric and look at the sexual crisis he faces in the experience of middle age.

While the female menopause is an established fact, there is no medical proof for a biological basis to a male "change of life." Nevertheless, middlescent males have reported any number of psychic symptoms such as impulsiveness, memory impairment, despondency and depression or excessive elation, a vague feeling of discontent or futility, sudden irrational fits of anger, unstable emotional reactions, and increased sexual desire or a tendency toward sexual impotence. In menopause the ovaries actually die a natural, functional death. No comparable biological change occurs in man, though the aging process brings a gradual decrease in various bodily secretions, in general muscle tone, and in energy and stamina. While it is true that the male sex hormone, androgen—produced by the adrenal cortex and testes—reaches a production peak at age twenty and declines gradually thereafter, this, taken by itself, should be no reason for the average, healthy man to push the panic button. Gradual, virtually imperceptible changes will eventually affect the copulatory responses in terms of frequency, intensity, duration, etc., *but* they by no means indicate that a male's ability to have intercourse is radically affected at middle age.

Another myth propagated by social convention is the idea that it is normal for men to lose interest in sex after a certain age. This is a case where thinking makes it so, where fear breeds fear. Or, as a prominent urologist declared, "What happens above a man's neck is vastly more important than what happens below his belt." [7] Researchers agree that there is no physical reason why a healthy man cannot continue to have intercourse well into his eighties.

Poor sexual performance with their wives (or at least the fear of it) is common among middle-aged men, but the vast majority of the causes are psychological. Achieving an erection is largely a psychological process which can be thwarted by various tensions or anxieties. And the more a man may worry about his potency, the more it will trouble him. In the recent research by William Masters and Virginia Johnson, which forms the basis for their report on *Human Sexual Inadequacy,* it was discovered that too often the impotent

[7] William Ferber, quoted by Frank, *Sexually Active Man,* p. 3.

male is not a concentrated participant in his own activity. He mentally steps outside and views himself as a detached spectator worrying about his performance and whether he will get an erection. The anxious wife does the same thing, and the sexual act is pulled out of its natural, playful context into an artificial arena in which both partners are worried spectators. The treatment that Masters and Johnson have found most helpful for such couples, therefore, is to encourage each spouse to explore way of giving and receiving bodily pleasure through sensory experiences. They make no initial demand for the couple to perform sexually until these touching, feeling, loving caresses awaken the natural desire to come together in the sexual act.

Of course, the various problems of the middlescent malaise form a vicious circle in relation to sexual functioning. For instance, the burden of business worries weighs heavily on the libido. One man avoided sexual relations with his wife when he was unable to find work, saying he "felt shriveled." Another man brought on a self-induced impotence because he was failing in his business and did not want to assume adult male responsibilities. Perhaps the most dramatic illustration of the interrelation between business and sex is seen in the studies made of the great stock market crash some years ago:

> Men who were worth fortunes on paper were wiped out, left penniless, overnight—in an hour. There was a grim joke among my older colleagues that the penises dropped faster than the stocks on Wall Street. We will never know how many men were made impotent temporarily by the crash. Six months later, it was routine to hear women say that they had had no sexual relations with their husbands since Black Thursday, the day the bottom fell out of the market.[8]

[8] Sophia J. Kleegman, gynecologist and past president of the American Association of Marriage Counselors, quoted by Stanley Frank, *Sexually Active Man*, p. 74.

It is apparent that one of the primary aids to the sexual rehabilitation of the man in the throes of his climacteric crisis is an understanding and reassuring wife. The best prescription is "TLC"—tender, loving care. Sometimes, however, a man who is impotent with his wife may mistake the erotic stimuli from a new liaison as the cure for his problem. As one person has noted, a lot of men would rather be accused of being unfaithful than being unable. So the man, failing in the sex act with his wife, discovers he is able to gain potency with a younger woman in an illicit affair. From this he deduces that the fault really lies with his wife, who no longer turns him on to sex. What he fails to realize, however, is that part of his newfound success is due to the fact that he is not required to copulate regularly with this new partner. If and when she is available to him every night he is likely to find himself back in the same boat, impotent and fearful of his fading masculinity.

Part of the problem of impotence in middle age rests in the widespread concern, typical of American men, over what is called "the numbers game," that is, how many times a week a man has intercourse. Good sex is a matter of quality rather than quantity, but many men have their sexual identity tied up with the number of times they are able to manage coitus. Various factors may affect such a schedule, including fatigue, tension, illness, and so forth, but if a man lags behind what he thinks is normal he may fear he is losing his sexual potency. That very psychological fear then impairs his performance far beyond the original, minor cause.

Some doctors lament the fact that nature has slipped up so badly in failing to complement the differences between the sexes in regard to sexual changes. The male reaches his peak of potency at age twenty or so and continues at a fairly consistent strong rate into the forties. Females, on the other hand, often reach their strongest sexual desire at forty and continue on a high level for another fifteen years or so. And, as we have noted, both sexes deal with the middle-age sexual

115

crisis at the same time. It seemed appropriate for a boy and girl to be of equal ages when they first fell in love and married, but now, a quarter of a century later, the woman's biological change and the man's psychological difficulties coincide. Too often the husband seeks to assuage his own guilt by pointing to real difficulties produced by his spouse, even though she is not responsible for the physical fate she is heir to in the menopause. Or she is blinded by a preoccupation with her own problems to understanding what is happening to her husband. In either case, the gap then grows and widens between them at a fast pace.

But perhaps this coincidence of middlescent difficulty can be the occasion for mutual help, providing that both partners understand their plight. The "Help Wanted" nature of this sexual crisis is not a play for getting back something lost in aging, but requires an understanding of the process and utilization of the force and strength that is basically there. If the husband can welcome his wife's increased ardor rather than fear it as a blow to his self-esteem, he can be restored to new realms of sexual enjoyment. Since the libido is a primary expression of the life force itself, the continuous cultivation of lovemaking through new forms of sensory stimulation will keep vitality surging in the later years.

Eating and sexual experience are probably two primary pleasures that are utterly renewable; that is, they are as enjoyable the thousandth time as the second, fifth, or twentieth time. Frequent intercourse through middle age builds up a continuous backlog of erotic memories, which in turn sustain the sexual responses as people get older. As middle-agers confront the menopause and climacteric, and ponder the question of whether to anticipate a continued interest in sex, they may be intrigued and amused by two observations on sex by the popular writer, Dr. David Reuben. For one thing, he points out that the events leading up to and involved in sexual intercourse are stimulating and recreational in themselves. As people get older and give up most of the activities of a vigorous life, copulation can continue to be an interesting and energizing pursuit, serving as an antidote to the isolation and depression. Second, for an exercise and weight-conscious public, Dr. Reuben describes the advantages of sexual intercourse in terms of sheer physical exercise and bodily health. Before and during orgasm the heart rate increases, the blood pressure rises for a short time (which is beneficial), and approximately 150 calories are consumed! Indeed, obviously with tongue-in-cheek, Dr. Reuben suggests that one act of intercourse is equal to half an hour of jogging, and that "once around the bed" is the exercise equivalent of running four times around the park. To these "practical" considerations regarding the continuance of intercourse, we may add that there are the important elements also of warmth, personal closeness to another person, intimacy, and loving affection, all of which are important at any age, but particularly in the crisis of midlife.

The menopause and climacteric both affect, and are affected by, the various difficulties of middlesence. But it is apparent that sexual relationships need not be suspended until everything else gets settled or until desire finally ceases. With a little bit of imagination marriage partners can make their sex life the beginning of a whole new phase in marriage beyond the previously destructive forms of the spouse gap. But it requires openness and willingness on the part of both partners.

LOST AND FOUND

Part of the suspense concerning sex during middlescence reflects the changing social mores of our day. As the well-worn cliché tells us, we are in an age of transition, and one of its revolutions concerns how people generally feel about sex and sexuality. In a sense, it is surprising that human beings are so preoccupied with sexual activity. We seem to be saturated in a sex-oriented, sensate society. Our stage shows, dramas, movies, and books are so explicit that one wonders what can follow for an encore—perhaps audience participation itself. Yet how could this interest be otherwise with a function recognized and described by Sigmund Freud to be "the most intensive pleasure of which man is capable." Is it not natural for man to seek and find the attainment of such enjoyment? No wonder many areas of inspiration in arts and science and psychic vitality find their source in this basic, driving life force we call sex. How can we think it odd that man should want to discover all he can about such a marvelous aspect of his own created being?

In short, we cannot ascribe such importance to sexual development and expression and then be surprised when people think it is important! Nor can we realistically expect that people with such promise of pleasurable and delightful feeling, will pursue sexual activity only within the safe confines of marriage.

This search for sexual fulfillment has particularly important implications for middlescence and for the spouse gap crisis. As we pick our way through the maze of changing social views on matters of sex, it is evident that contemporary man has lost something and has found something in terms of his sexual status. It is important for middle-agers to sort through the lost and found by being open to the experience around them and by appropriating those elements which may help alleviate some of their difficulties.

What has been lost is, essentially, the interpersonal dimension of sexual relationships. The more we are excessively preoccupied with sex as the key to our own identity, the less we seem to be in touch with our basic sexuality and personhood. Rather than cultivating a personal relationship in which the sex act may become one of the elements of expression, we have a tendency to think in terms of our own desirability, technique, and satisfaction. Here the numbers game thrives. Sex becomes a sensation on which we feed, only to find that it offers temporary relief, with little nourishment for the whole person.

Our technological and moralistic culture has tended to encourage the widespread repression of sensory feelings in us. Thus in the subsequent wasteland of emptiness, boredom, and loneliness we often fly to sexual relationships to try to prove to ourselves that we can feel and that we do have feelings. Such flight may be, for men, an attempt to preserve flagging feelings of masculinity by piling up conquests through the pride of "scoring." For women the search may be for the elusive experience of a bigger and better orgasm. Here Dr. Reuben cautions that if orgasm could be considered the ultimate goal of sex, then masturbation would be the ideal, since it is simpler and cheaper than other ways of achieving orgasm. Yet, it lacks the crucial ingredient of emotional involvement, and, without emotional feeling, sex soon becomes deprived of physical feeling as well. To use the new sexual freedom as a license to copulate in a passionless, almost mechanical attitude makes the partner an "it"—an impersonal object necessary for one's own ego-trip gratification.

Much in the current scene tends to foster this climate of permissiveness. Sexuality has been ruthlessly commercialized to sell everything imaginable. Ad men rack their brains to come up with the double-meaning jingle, whether it's for shaving cream ("take it off, take it all off"), alcohol, cigarettes ("It's not how long you make it; it's how you make it long"), or potato chips. The ads are designed to convey the message that sex is for the young and the beautiful—ergo! anyone can become young and beautiful by doing it (and buying the product, of course). And everything is to be gotten immediately, without waiting, instant coffee, instant relief from headache pain, instant sex. To make a conquest, satisfy oneself and one's partner with as little wasted effort on activities unrelated to sex as possible, and move on makes sex a kind of drug, a tranquilizer which dulls the very feeling

119

it seeks to acquire. Such fleeting liaisons, no matter how erotically stimulating at the moment, only serve to intensify the sense of isolation and aloneness when once the pleasure has passed and the partners have parted.

Furthermore, the *Playboy* philosophy of sex is all based on the impersonal, hygienic, skillful cultivation of the aura of sexuality while omitting personal considerations and human interaction. We have only to look at the mindless and emotionless bodies and the vacuous expressions on the faces of the fold-out "Playmates" to wonder, with Rollo May, whether Hugh Hefner has not shifted "the fig leaf from the genitals to the face." Rarely in all the sex-saturated literature, advertising, TV programs, and movies do we see a homely girl. Yet there is more truth than poetry in Harry Golden's remarks that some of the world's most beautiful loving has been done by homely women. Despite their public image contrived by press agents, sex symbols and glamour girls do not necessarily have the inner warmth and sensitivity which make the sexual relationship a loving or lovely experience.

Certainly there is an important element of self-discovery in the sex act which gives pleasure and arouses sensations, and which tells how it feels to be a partner in this intimate human relationship. But such elements of self-gratification, implicit as they are in intercourse, cannot be divorced from the interpersonal quality of the lovemaking without destroying the emotional and human dimension of the experience.

Consider one of the characters in John Updike's best-selling novel of love, marriage, and adultery in America, *Couples*. Piet Hanema, the studdiest yet the most pathetic figure among the couples of the New England community of Tarbox, hops from one affair to another. It is true that his wife is sexually indifferent (a kind of unreachable Iseult figure from the Tristan myth), and that other women are eager and willing to go to bed with him. Yet Piet's search for life through sex is strongly motivated by a spiritual confusion, a sense of fleeting time and a fear of death. However, the more he copulates, the more insatiable is his sexual need, until he discovers and uses a streak of cruelty in himself as a new source of pleasure. In bed with one of his partners Piet suddenly slaps her several times. Then, the passage goes on:

> Seeing her eyes incredulous, he had slapped her again, to banish all doubt and establish them firmly on this new frontier. Already he had exploited her passivity in all positions; the slap distracted his penis and he felt he had found a method to prolong the length of time, never long enough, that he could inhabit a woman.[9]

For Piet Hanema, as for his friends, preoccupation with sex led to a new cult of hedonism in which anything goes, even hurting the partner if it adds to one's own pleasure. For others, the cult of hedonism leads to sexual cruelties that include whipping, torture, punishment, and other forms of extreme sadomasochistic sex behavior. The loss of personal and affectional relatedness in such sexual liaisons is obvious.

Integral to ultimate fulfillment in sexual relationships is the experience of love and desire as a mutual seduction, the outpouring of feeling between a man and woman who want to gratify each other and to find themselves more whole and more human in that relationship together. Surely this mutuality is clear when we consider the very reciprocal nature of the sex act: what enhances or hinders pleasure for one person directly affects the other. Getting in touch with this interpersonal quality is a large part of the real enjoyment of sex. The biblical term for sexual intercourse is generally translated "to know." To know another person in the intimacy of intercourse is the way in which we can know ourselves as sexual human beings.

What has been lost in present-day sex mores, then, has to do essentially with the qualities of warmth, fidelity, lovingness, and livingness of the other person. The sex drive itself

---

[9] John Updike, *Couples* (New York: A Fawcett Crest Book, 1968), p. 352.

is impersonal, and crude sex can find relief with little mutuality and personal interaction. But human beings yearn for more than this. To seek communion with another without a context of a loving relationship will fail, for "a man is never more alone than when he is locked in a loveless sexual embrace." [10] This lostness can infect the marriage bed as well as any other, and may be one of the present attitudes contributing to the spouse gap.

But let us also look at what has been found in sex in the light of our changing sexual mores. Basically we find ourselves in a general climate of opinion which allows us to say "yes" to our own sexuality, to affirm our sexual impulses and our enjoyment of sexual relationship as a natural and good part of our created natures. At last women can acknowledge their sexual feelings without being judged as endowed with unnatural sex drives. No longer is sex sanctified simply because it is the vehicle of procreation. Sex is being recognized as a vital source of loving communication between a man and woman that can be enjoyed for its own sake.

It is puzzling why we have so long tried to hide, or rationalize, or explain away the pleasure that comes in lovemaking, as though our sexual organs were not part of our total beings. Again, Dr. Reuben makes this point clear by pointing out that each of us has traveled that seven-inch distance "through the penis into the vagina to meet the other half of our future protoplasm, and has then settled in the uterus for the 280-day wait." He then says that any shame we may feel about that journey and the place of our subsequent development is unfounded, for "there is no more suitable place."

In spite of all our "adults only" movies, books, and magazines, and all our manuals on techniques, most of us have remained quite coy about sex. We have regarded the genitals with secrecy and gained our knowledge in a kind of game of

[10] Frank, *The Sexually Active Man*, p. 222.

"hide and peek." Now, perhaps, we will be able to reorder our sexual values openly in the daylight. Too much of the idea that sex is "dirty" or "forbidden" has been nourished in the dark cellars of social taboo and then twisted by exploiters into something sensational which would arouse and titillate the commercial voyeur.

We are discovering, also, that sexual activity has a kind of energy and creative self-expression that is a form of play. Not play as mere idle, frivolous merriment or the cynical use of another person as a thing, but play in the sense of sheer spontaneity for mutual satisfaction, sex as a joy and end in itself. Intercourse need not be just serious work to beget children or to fulfill a conjugal duty, or even to create companionship. The sex act is an expression of the joyful sharing of life. As a Roman Catholic lay theologian writes in a provocative piece entitled, "Frequent, Even Daily, Communion":

> For love-making is an act of the human person, of intelligence and sensitivity, of gentleness and respect for one another, of struggle and of happy combat. The whole psyche is involved in it: one's skin, one's emotions, one's juices, one's mind, one's perceptions, one's freedom, one's aspirations. Animals have babies, but they do not make love. Human beings create an art of playfulness and make love, not when they need to, but when they wish. It is those who make love only in order to have children who mechanize and dehumanize the act of intercourse.[11]

In this sense the changing mores are freeing us to enjoy sex as a gift rather than an achievement, as an experience of play rather than an accomplishment of work.

Along with finding the element of play in sex we are discovering that maybe we have made sex a more serious preoccupation than it need be. As we noted, the sex drive itself

[11] Michael Novak, "Frequent, Even Daily, Communion," *The Catholic Case for Contraception,* ed. Daniel Callahan (London: Macmillan & Co., 1969) , p. 98.

pulses through the whole natural world of which man is a part. To try to pry all manifestations of that force into what we know as the experience of love has led us into all kinds of mental gymnastics. There is something laughable in what the power of sheer sexual desire can do to a person. To assume that every time we are sexually aroused it is a matter for serious reflection is to lose perspective on ourselves. Tom Driver suggests that we have a lot to learn from looking at the humor in sex. Not the lewd-snicker or embarrassed-giggle variety of humor, but the healthy, commonsense variety that tells us sex is necessary but is not necessity itself:

> Laughter at sex is about the only way to put sex in its place, to assert one's humanity over against that impersonal, irrational, yet necessary force that turns even the best of men into caricatures of themselves. Not only "sinful" sex does this: lawful sex, safely within the limits of marriage and love, does it too, as everybody knows; and he who does not laugh about it must be humiliated by it.[12]

The ability to see our sexual selves in such perspective can lead us into a new spirit of delight, affirmation, and honesty in relation to ourselves and our partners. This is especially important to discover in middle age when the implications of our sexual relationships are distorted by so many other factors. How neat it would be if we could stop worrying about sex and just relax and enjoy the revolution!

This is not to say that the emerging "New Morality" will or should condone "free love" or promiscuous sex. Nothing truly creative can ever happen without discipline, and sex, being but one aspect of the total life, must find its proportionate place in a man or woman if he or she is to find wholeness and fulfillment as a person and not fall prey to the antinomian syndrone. Sex and lovemaking alone soon

[12] Tom F. Driver, "On Taking Sex Seriously," *Christianity and Crisis*, October 14, 1963, p. 177.

pales and withers—it must not only feed the rest of life, but be fed by it as well. Sexual relations are not only present, but part of a past and future as well; not only private, but also part of a community. "The logic of the Liebestod is impeccable," Sidney Callahan comments, "man cannot live by sex alone. The lovers in *Elvira Madigan* and other romantic fables bore us to death before they finally get around to suicide." [13] The play and pleasure elements in sexual relationships are made more vital when part of a well-rounded, wider life experience.

To the extent that many middle-agers have been raised on a strict view of sex as work and duty, they may readily agree with the above observations on the place of discipline in sex. Their need, however, may be to mix freedom with discipline. The spouse gap in middlescence, at least as far as sex is concerned, can best be breached sometimes if the partners can lay hold on this new freedom and spirit of play in order to swing across the gap.

The element of suspense regarding sex still remains as we turn from analysis and interpretation to experience. Will what has been found today about sex outweigh what has been lost, or vice versa? At this point we can only mention the possibilities. Middlescent couples who are plagued by the malaise of their time of life can find the changing mores regarding sex impinging on their relationship at numerous places. If the sex-saturation of commercialization takes the upper hand, spouses may see their partners receding further beyond the gap into impersonal "things" that either function or do not function properly as sex partners. If, however, the message comes home to the couple that sex is to be enjoyed by them together as an end in itself, that it is an appropriate form of adult play, that it is a delightful and astonishing arena for communication, they may be on their way to a new closeness. What they express and communicate to each other

[13] Sidney Callahan, "Human Sexuality in a Time of Change," *The Christian Century* (August 28, 1968), p. 1079.

may still be in question, but their realization that they are free to explore together is half the battle.

Sexual relations in middle age, then, can become an important springboard into the wider vistas of human meaning. It can grow into maturity and meaning to rekindle the incendiary powers of love. Bertrand Russell expresses this beautifully in his autobiography:

> I have sought love, first, because it brings ecstasy—ecstasy so great that I would often have sacrificed all the rest of life for a few hours of this joy. I have sought it, next, because it relieves loneliness—that terrible loneliness in which one shivering consciousness looks over the rim of the world into the cold unfathomable lifeless abyss. I have sought it, finally, because in the union of love I have seen, in a mystic miniature, the prefiguring vision of the heaven that saints and poets have imagined. This is what I sought, and though it might seem too good for human life, this is what—at last —I have found.[14]

Suspense of this kind within the marriage-life drama is an experience to which we might all aspire. For Russell, in the long run, all was found and nothing lost in his sense of the sustaining power of love and the goodness of human sexuality. And he made his observations long after he passed middle age!

[14] *The Autobiography of Bertrand Russell* (London: Allen & Unwin, 1967).

V

CRISIS: SPOUSE GAP ESCALATION

The second act of our marriage drama now gathers momentum and propels us into a major crisis period. Here the middlescent malaise exacts its toll from the marital relationship itself. Instead of giving mutual aid and comfort in time of desperate need, marriage mates sometimes bug each other in ugly discontent, or ignore each other in utter disregard. In a Detroit study of marriage, researchers Blood and Wolfe discovered that 52 percent of the wives were very satisfied with their marriages during the first two years, but only 6 percent were still satisfied twenty years later and 21 percent "were very dissatisfied." [1] The middlescent malaise gnaws away at the marriage structure, making little forgotten gaps bigger and creating new gaps where none existed before.

Middle-age crisis time is a time of buck-passing, of blaming the other person, of finding fault, of jockeying for the best position in the marriage-go-round. One peculiarly interesting observation about this game is that the husband can call his wife a bitch or a shrew, the wife can call her husband a clod or a bully, and yet neither one remembers that this is the same dear person he or she *chose* to marry. It is easy at this point to forget that both have contributed their assets and liabilities to the marriage pattern, enforcing certain grooves and modes of behavior either consciously or unconsciously. Now, since it takes as much or more effort to keep a bad relationship going as it does a good one, we find many middle-agers spinning their wheels, expending a

[1] Blood, *Marriage*, pp. 201-2.

lot of their energy for nothing: building defenses, gathering ammunition, planning an attack strategy, and rationalizing that the spouse is the enemy, rather than "facing it like it is" and examining the pattern of interaction which left the marriage door open to gaposis during these rough years of middlescence.

This crisis time is also the time for what is described by Ken Kesey, in his novel *Sometimes a Great Notion*, as the "go-away-closer disease." The husband or wife may be starving for contact with the spouse, but avoids contact like poison when it is offered. He or she may long for human relatedness, but ends up sabotaging any chance for it to happen. Barriers are erected to keep anyone from getting too close, too intimate, too involved—yet the person is unhappy and restless in isolation.

How does one catch this strange "go-away-closer disease"? Well, it seems to come, in varying degrees, with the middlescent malaise. The anger or frustration or disappointment we feel about the world and what it has done to us (or prevented us from doing) is directed at the person with whom we live in closest proximity. It is another form of kicking the cat. We may sense that things have gone awry, but for some reason find it impossible to talk about the situation with our spouse. The next step is to stop ourselves from caring about, or feeling for, or doing as much for the other person because our own problems require all our attention. It is hard to be sensitive to the needs of our spouse if we are locked in our own inner struggles. Besides, since no one else really understands us, we must keep our defenses up lest we reveal more than we want to show. Who wants someone else knowing what we are *really* like down inside, the resentments, the hurts, the frustration, the failures?

People afflicted by the "go-away-closer disease" are, of course, lonely. It always comes as a surprise to single persons to discover that loneliness can exist in a relationship as intimate as marriage, but this phenomenon is far from unusual. Couples separated by travel, business, or health may be lonely, but these factors in themselves are not the chief contributors to a gut-level sense of loneliness which means real marital difficulty. There is, rather, a kind of deep debilitating loneliness, an estrangement which is often found within the conjugal lives of middle-aged couples who are living together at close range. This loneliness is characterized not by mere physical absence, but by silence, boredom, and lack of personal sharing.

Crisis time in middlescence is also the time for a general loss of intimacy. Couples don't keep up with each other and thus grow apart as the individual partners change. We once supposed that the longer two people lived together, the more they became alike. But this is being questioned by current research experience. In fact, the early will toward agreement tends to become difficult to maintain as new issues arise and a general decline in consensus sets in over the years. By itself this fact need not destroy the solidarity of the marriage, but where the spouses do not talk about it or listen to each other, there is a corresponding loss of intimacy as the consensus falls away.

Intimacy is lost also as spouses begin to see each other's faults more glaringly. Over the years faults may come to loom larger as virtues turn into vices and then, in the throes of the middlescent malaise, become blatantly intolerable. Here again, spouses usually show a reluctance to discuss the unpleasant aspects of each other's personalities—except, perhaps, in the heat of anger when they couch them in derogatory terms that question the partner's sanity or intelligence. Such an approach usually ruffles feathers and speeds up the spouse-gap escalation.

This discussion does not mean to imply that the presence of intimacy in a marriage can be determined by whether the two partners "tell all" to each other about everything. Stable companionship and true intimacy do not rest on detailed confessions or intrusions into privacy, but on a basic trust and wholehearted commitment to the process of interaction and communication. Intimacy does involve a balance in personal relationship which prevents it from becoming a burden to either or both partners. When intimacy fades or is experienced as a burden, the marriage may eventually fall apart. If intimacy simply goes down the drain through lack of attention, the marriage may one day break up on the rocks of loneliness and neglect.

Intimacy must often be fought for. Witness the case of George and Helen. Before marrying they spent long, leisurely hours together, planned trips, talked about their future. After they were married, they both carried a heavy work load and discovered that opportunities to talk freely together were rare. Over the years this routine hardened and they finally realized they were growing apart. One day George remarked somewhat ruefully, "If I want to talk to my wife alone, I have to make an appointment a week ahead!" Helen, overhearing his words, replied with equal irony, "Why dear, we pass on the stairs now and then!" Fortunately George and Helen brought some perspective to bear on their predicament and started to "make time" for being alone together, no matter how difficult.

But for every George and Helen there are countless couples who know they are victims of a gap, but don't seem to make the effort to get back together. They just drift farther and farther apart. We are reminded of the odd couple that Eugene Ionesco depicts with irony in his play *The Bald Soprano*. In one scene a man and woman happen to meet and engage in polite, somewhat mannered conversation. As they talk they discover they both came down to New York that morning on the 10:00 train, and they both have the same apartment house address on Fifth Avenue. To their surprise they discover they both also live in the same apartment and both have a daughter seven years old. To their final astonishment they discover they are man and wife! They live together, share the same bed and the same kitchen table, but intimacy has fled from their relationship, leaving them strangers.

Whenever difficulties arise in marriage, there is a deep-seated temptation to withdraw elsewhere rather than hang in with the mate. One psychiatrist describes it this way:

The woman longs to carry her troubles to her nearest woman friend for sympathy and comfort because her great need is on the feeling side and it takes an act of conscious determination to stay and work on the problem with her husband. The man is tempted to fling off and seek out another woman in order to find his sexual satisfaction in a temporary affair where the conditions are not so difficult, but where his obligation can be met by some material gift and where, above all, no intolerable demand is made to talk things over and to understand.[2]

At no time is this temptation more strongly felt than in middlescence. Doubts, loneliness, loss of intimacy, the onslaught of the "go-away-closer disease"—all these feelings seem to indicate it is *easier* to deal with problems separately than to weather the storm that comes from dealing with them together.

But there are important areas within middle age where marriage mates must "face it like it is" side by side in mutual interaction—critical places which affect both partners deeply. Unless a couple meets these together the spouse gap cannot help escalating into an ugly ditch across their marriage landscape. Here, then, we will turn to look at three crisis areas: (1) what happens when the children grow up and leave home, The Empty Nest; (2) how the job market looks to the middle-aged, Business as Unusual; and (3) the retreat into excessive drinking and the advance into extramarital affairs, Galloping Gaposis and the Lure of Adultery.

[2] Harding, *Way of All Women,* p. 328.

THE EMPTY NEST

We all remember the romantic fable which ends with a wedding and the line "and they lived happily ever after." Well, happily or not, ever after is a much longer period today than it used to be. Even fifty years ago, perhaps one parent was deceased by the time the last child married. And the parent still living anticipated going to live with one of the children when no longer able to live alone.

Today, however, with earlier marriages, fewer children, better health, and increased longevity, a couple may have almost as many years together without children in the home as they had with them. Whether these prove to be bonus years for the couple or simply an extended prison sentence depends on how the partners face the middle-age crisis called nest-emptying, a major transition point marking middlescence.

Studies show that when the last child grows up and leaves home there is an increased likelihood of marital maladjustment. This event acts as a kind of marital catalyst, demanding that husband and wife face themselves, each other, and their marriage in a way they have never had to before. And the longer they avoid this task, the faster the gap between them widens.

For one thing, when the children leave, the couple must make profound adjustments in their parental and spouse roles. This is especially true for the mother who has devoted herself so completely to her children that she is left with the feeling of being abandoned, and thus unloved and uncared for. When her children grow up the mother literally joins the ranks of the unemployed, where she may begin to sense that she has little reason or justification for her life, little value or worth as a contributor to the process of living. She may experience "post-parental depression" and share the feeling of the mother who said she "felt like dying" when her last daughter got married.

So the experience of the "empty nest" is always something of a crisis. It leaves a devastating sense of emptiness and purposelessness. The silent house is full of memories. There was once so much to do, and now there is so little. The crowded, busy years seemed arduous at the time. But now, looking back, it is clear that this was far outweighed by the deep, solid satisfaction of being needed.[3]

The groundwork for this traumatic experience for women is embedded in the conventional notion that in a good marriage the woman lives only for the collective values of being a wife and mother, with emphasis on the latter task since most of the care for the children falls on her shoulders. If she worked before marriage she usually was expected to put all that behind her upon entering the wedded state. Even if she continued to work after marrying, she was expected to do so without neglecting her family duties. With such an expectation, it is no wonder that the woman, particularly the one who has devoted her life exclusively to motherhood, should undergo a terrific psychological change when all her children are gone. Rooms that once rocked with loud laughter and louder music are now strangely silent and still.

The father must also readjust to the empty nest, of course, but his job and other outside interests usually occupy his attention. Since he has not been as directly and constantly related to the children, his adjustment is less radical. Indeed he may even breathe a sigh of relief when the children are finally out on their own. As they grew up, the mother's actual work load got somewhat lighter, but he felt increasing pressures for bigger allowances, more clothes, money for college, money to get started with a career or new home. Now, at last, he can feel some relief. Though it is also possible that when he does let up he will experience something of the same loss his wife does, that he is no longer needed,

[3] Mace, *Success in Marriage*, pp. 102-3.

he is less important, he has been replaced, and the offspring can no longer be treated as children.

But for the wife in particular, now freed from the cares and concerns of child rearing, the empty-nest crisis represents a turning point in her life as she confronts the need to decide what to do with her life and future, perhaps another quarter century of good years yet. Now, more than ever, the bored housewife feels trapped and incarcerated in the split-level dream house. If the family has sufficient financial resources she may attempt those creative pursuits she dreamed of but for which there was never enough time—painting, writing, reading, travel, etc. But unless such interests have been maintained at some minimal level she is likely to find either the flesh or the spirit lacking. She is afraid to try something new again. Community colleges are finding that increasing numbers of "ex" mothers enroll for college extension courses in subjects that interest them. If family resources are available, and her spouse is understanding, these pursuits can lead the woman into new discoveries of meaning and give her a new sense of self-esteem as an individual in her own right.

More than likely, however, the unemployed mother will seek some kind of work, especially if she has a job before or at some time during her marriage. When a person's inner sense of worth has broken down, there is a tendency to look for some tangible, objective indication that he or she still has value in the world. For the person who is work-oriented, a paycheck may provide some such assurance, if only temporarily. Under these circumstances the woman who is unsuccessful in getting a job may feel an even greater sense of failure and uselessness.

On the other hand, if the woman is successful in finding employment, a whole new set of problems may arise: Does she keep her salary for herself, put it into the household, or divide it some way between the two? Does her working constitute a threat to her husband's ego or add to his growing self-doubts? Does her job require her to be gone from home when he is there? Does the stimulation of the new job and the glamour of meeting new people lead her to seek her pleasures outside her marriage, thus increasing the growing spouse gap?

One of the primary consequences of the empty-nest crisis is often sheer loneliness. The woman has to find some kind of activity or reenter the labor market to fill those long, silent hours. This was less a problem in earlier years when families lived closer together, providing mutual support and extended security as well as company. But post–World War II America took to the road and families became increasingly scattered. Couples move so much they often fail to put down roots; neighborhoods do not provide easy access to friends and the nuclear family unit seems alone in the midst of an urban or suburban wilderness. Now let the children leave as the parents are dealing with their own middlescent malaise, and a loneliness crisis crops up.

Let us consider the specific case of John and Pauline. John is a vice-president, chief engineer, and troubleshooter for a large construction and ocean-oriented firm with projects all over the world. He met Pauline in college, and they married just prior to the end of World War II. She worked briefly as a legal secretary but quit before the wedding to become a full-time wife and, subsequently, mother. To outsiders, John and Pauline have had an ideal marriage. They have three children, two boys and a girl in the middle, each born two years after the previous one. John is very successful in his work and travels extensively. The family has lived for extended periods of time in both Europe and South America. Educated at the best schools in various countries, the children can speak several languages and have friends all over the world.

At this point, however, Pauline is facing a personal crisis. Her whole life has centered around her family—making a home and getting everyone taken care of wherever they lived, making herself available to her husband for whatever new task might be thrust upon him, and generally co-ordinating schedules, packing, unpacking, entertaining. John is a good father and very attentive to his wife and children when with them. But the truth is that most of the care and rearing of the kids has been up to Pauline. She has done a good job: the older two are both happily married, one out of college and the other still attending with her husband. The youngest is finishing high school and will then go off to college. In other words, Pauline's "nest" will soon be empty.

The way of life for John, Pauline, and family has been one of affection and consideration, but also of self-sufficiency and independence. Pauline now is face to face with the fact that in one more year her job as mother ends. She suddenly feels panic-stricken. Always there has been some trip to plan, some child to meet, extra beds to be found for the children's friends. Before her she sees only long, lonely hours in a strange country waiting for John to return from a special assignment.

John has promised Pauline that they will settle down in a few years, but in the meantime her future looks bleak. She would like to return to school, but can't be sure she could be in one place long enough to take any courses. She has thought of returning to work, but finds that posing the same schedule problem, plus the fact that she has a haunting sense that she is no longer qualified or competent to work in the business world.

Furthermore, Pauline now finds that she really resents being so completely dependent on John. He has always taken care of their financial matters, giving her money as she needed it. While she resents that arrangement, they have operated that way so long that she is afraid to say so and risk rocking their marital boat. Pauline admires and respects John very much, and has heretofore enjoyed the glamour of being his wife. But, in reality, her children were her real companions as John darted here and there on business. Now the children are all pursuing their own lives with no more need of her in those old terms, and her time and energy need to be redirected as she now faces having a sizable block of free time on her hands. Now, each trip is merely a task to be endured rather than a holiday or a problem she has to solve. Even the thought of a home of her own seems empty and hollow to Pauline. So far John suspects nothing, but Pauline fears she may not be able to pretend much longer.

The case of John and Pauline puts the crisis of the empty nest in bold relief. It is a time of stress and testing for both of them, though John has not yet confronted the crisis created by the children's growing up and leaving home, nor faced the widening spouse gap between him and Pauline. Their life circumstances have changed, and adjustments in their roles will have to be met in one way or another.

Some women, more insecure and dependent perhaps than Pauline, confront their empty nests and refuse to accept what they see. Instead, they cling to their children and won't let them go. They lavish their children with gifts and affection and indulgences and butt in on their budding families, as though pathetically hoping to earn some attention and gratitude in return. In short, they become problem mothers-in-law, so that the in-law is considered an out-law.

This kind of reaction calls for great understanding on the part of the spouse and the children. If a mother has for years given up everything for her daughter, focusing on providing her with the best opportunities in education, social activities, and suitors, she is bound to take it hard when the daughter marries and moves away. She usually has the best intentions in visiting her daughter at every opportunity, and taking her grandchildren on extended visits and spoiling them. But behind these actions may be a loneliness and dependence on the offspring which can escalate the gap between her and her spouse. The overly mothering wife—that is, the woman who has not developed her own self as a whole person, but only as a mother—actually fails to be a good mother. She is unable to do what the good mother must: learn to play a new role; let go of her children, painful as that may be; and recognize her children's autonomy.

The close emotional ties that parents have with their children can be seen in a curious phenomenon noted by Stanley Frank. He describes cases in which a husband may unconsciously curtail sexual intercourse with his wife out of worry that his son might get a girl pregnant and be forced into marriage, and in which a mother may do the same out of fear that her daughter is having a premarital affair. Then Frank notes the reaction of some couples to their child's marriage:

> Their rate of intercourse drops after the wedding and remains low until it picks up again with the arrival of a grandchild. They have read so many stories about sexual maladjustments among young people that anxiety over the stability of a child's marriage curbs their own desire for coitus. The birth of a baby proves only that a man and a woman slept together once, of course, but it seems to give the grandparents assurance that the newlyweds' sexual relationship is mutually satisfactory.[4]

In this case the nest may be empty but the implications of the nesting instinct linger on.

By far the worst consequence of the empty-nest crisis is the shock some couples get when they confront each other alone and realize they don't know each other at all. This may happen especially in a marriage where the couple have used the children as their primary way of relating to each other or as a buffer between them on points of conflict. When the children leave home the spouses, in their psychological nakedness, confront each other across the gap which has always been between them and which was temporarily filled by their children.

[4] Frank, *Sexually Active Man*, p. 136.

In answer to the question on our Interview Schedule, "What would you say is the best thing about your marriage?", a number of the respondents said "our children." One wonders what their response will be when the children are no longer there as the center of their marital lives.

The early years of marriage, as we have said, are focused around the children. After some twenty years or so, and the children having been launched, marriage undergoes a radical loss of purpose. The couple confront each other as strangers. Suddenly the husband sees his wife as a lady with gray in her hair and wrinkles. The wife sees her husband as dreary, overweight, balding; and each says to himself, "My God, who are you?" To the couple facing one another without children as intermediaries, the poverty of personal resources is revealed in bold relief. Instead of turning to each other to build a new and better life together, the partners frequently drift apart and go their separate ways, into alcoholism, extra-marital affairs, or various forms of neurotic behavior. Were they able to see themselves confronting the crisis of the empty nest, they could give each other the comfort needed and create a renewed companionship that would enrich the middle and later years. One writer offers this possibility:

> Husbands and wives can help each other through the child-leaving stage by recognizing, supporting, and sharing each other's need to mourn. The emptying nest brings genuine grief with its constellation of many feelings—sadness, resentment, guilt, emptiness, and depression. Each partner must do his "grief work"—the work of his personality in letting go of the children emotionally, accepting the reality of their leaving and dealing with the varied feelings these events bring.[5]

Both spouses must adjust to new roles as their children leave home, but the trauma is usually greatest for the woman.

[5] Howard J. Clinebell, Jr., and Charlotte H. Clinebell, *The Intimate Marriage* (New York: Harper and Row, 1970), p. 128.

In the next middlescent crisis area to be looked at, however, we find the greatest impact is on the man.

BUSINESS AS UNUSUAL

While the wife is trying to cope with being a middle-aged, unemployed mother, the husband is usually engaged in the battle of being meaningfully and gainfully employed. Becoming middlescent is inevitable, but for some it means coping with an occupational crisis. If being in the "middle" implies that everything to come is on a downhill, descending path, such recognition brings a great shock to most men in relation to their jobs or to their general position in the business world. The emotional, psychological, and physical adaptation to that initial shock profoundly affects the marital relationship and may escalate the spouse gap.

Men who attain high-echelon, executive rank usually gain that achievement at a time coinciding with the onslaught of middle age. Within a relatively short time after arriving at the position for which he fought so hard, therefore, the man must begin preparing some younger rival to take over. The very name of this game is "prepare your successor." Such a shift in focus from a competitive thrust to a selfless regard for the business brings built-in strains on the ego. A vague feeling dawns on one that not only machines but people—especially middle-aged people—become obsolescent.

The depressive effect of the middlescent malaise on one may reflect a growing sense of disillusionment concerning work itself. Earlier idealism having long been shattered, there is now a tendency to lose the impulse for action-oriented behavior and to face the sobering realization that people are not innately good. By mid-life, one finds that working with people has made it clear that removing obstacles to better conditions does not bring an accompanying change in human nature, that people have an inexhaustible capacity for destruction as well as for creative, loving behavior. With such disillusionment the middlescent may simply try to keep conflict at a minimum, to keep everything nice and quiet—in other words, to not rock the boat or make waves.

Of course the middlescent crisis can be an occasion for growth and maturity in one's perspective on work. When that happens the man becomes a very valuable resource to the business, as well as a more satisfied person to himself and his family. As he gets older, the man may discover new sources of creativity, which, together with his accumulated experience and knowledge over the years, makes his contribution more profound and technically efficient. The younger man may be more flashy, more impulsive, more daring—and also more ego-centered. Weathering the tempering effect of middle age can leave the older man with more concern for the business as a whole, or for social causes beyond himself, or for renewed evaluation of long-range human values in the business world.

For those who doubt the ability of older men to provide any significant contribution to mankind, consider the following list of accomplishments:

> Sophocles, who lived to be more than 90, wrote *Oedipus Rex* at 75, and *Oedipus et Colonus* at 89. Titian completed his masterpiece, "The Battle of Lepanto," at 95; he began work on one of the most famous paintings in the world, "The Descent from the Cross," when he was 97. Benjamin Franklin invented bifocals at 78. Benjamin Duggar, Professor of Plant Physiology and Botanical Economics at the University of Wisconsin, was removed at age 70 by compulsory retirement; he then joined the research staff of Lederle Laboratories and several years later gave mankind Aureomycin. At 90, Pablo Casals still played the cello as no other man ever had. Santayana, the philosopher, wrote his first novel, *The Last Puritan,* at 72. Carl Sandburg wrote

141

Remembrance Rock at 70. Freud's activities continued into his 80's.[6]

Some of the world's greatest feats come from people long after they have passed middle age. So there is no reason to believe that a person suddenly loses his competency and ability when he reaches the "ripe" age of 35 or 40. But if he panics and fights changes out of fear, it is likely his self-confidence and his performance will suffer and will cause him to feel that he no longer has the stuff required of him.

The present generation of middle-agers has, for the most part, been raised on the pablum of the work ethic. Admit it or not, that is our hang-up. We have measured our worth by our work. Not only have we been told that a job is necessary in order for us to have the essentials (and then the luxuries) of life, but we have been conditioned to believe it is necessary to our very survival as human beings in an acquisitive society. We are firmly convinced that hard work is the royal road to success. Some seek work as an outlet for aggression; others see work as a necessity for disciplining the mind and the spirit. For others, work has been regarded as necessary for man's salvation, since idleness gives rise to mischief, and other devilish delights.

While these conventional views of work have been tempered somewhat in recent times, particularly with the new-leisure revolution,[7] a person still gains a primary sense of identity and self-worth through his work. Thus any hint of failure, whether by error in judgment or technological unemployment, or by becoming middle-aged, may drive its victim into depression and/or illness. Upon entering middlescence, therefore, a man may react to his job in any of a variety of ways: he may strive to work and compete harder and longer than ever before to prove he is still of worth.

[6] Harry Levinson, "On Being a Middle-Aged Manager," *Harvard Business Review*, July-August 1969, p. 52.

[7] See Robert Lee, *Religion and Leisure in America* (Nashville: Abingdon Press), 1964.

Or he may give way to disillusionment, recognizing that his work has not brought him satisfaction, and simply drop out of the whole scene to bum around. Or he may decide to change vocations and try to find himself in something he really wants to do. In any event, the middle-ager rarely continues with "business as usual"—business as "unusual" is a more apt description.

If a man reacts to the middlescent malaise by pushing himself ever more on the job, he is usually headed for a serious state of tension or breakdown. Consider this description from an article in *Time:*

> On the surface, he is a successful executive at Kaiser Industries, 40 years old, with important responsibilities. But he worries constantly about whether he is equal to the job. More often than not, a routine phone call from a superior sets off a sudden, stabbing pain in his chest. Company doctors are seriously concerned about his health. Constant tension, they report, brings on the pains of angina pectoris, which often precede a heart attack.[8]

The man in an executive or managerial position in particular will feel not only his inner pressure to perform and to excel, but the unending competitive pressure that goes with his job responsibility. While the workweek is declining for industrial laborers, more and more executives are working longer hours, more days a week.

Observing the increased psychic pressures and the consequent rash of peptic ulcers among his patients, a certain doctor was moved to offer some tongue-in-cheek advice to compulsive, work-driven, middlescent managers.

—Think only of your job. Your wife and children love you for what you are doing and understand why they never see you.

---

[8] "The Rising Pressures to Perform," *Time*, July 18, 1969, p. 75.

—Spend holidays and weekends at the office while the family goes to the mountains or the seashore, so you can work in peace and quiet.

—Attend all the business meetings and conferences and serve on all the committees you can. Speak at any gathering on any subject, if you think it will help you to a promotion or give your career a boost.

—Don't waste your time on recreation. Always include business associates in your golf foursome or luncheon group.

—Keep your attaché case with you at all times so you can use any free time to go over business problems.

—Plan any business trips at night so you can put in a full day at the office, fly or drive to your destination, and still keep early appointments the next day.

—Don't depend on anyone but yourself to get the job done. Don't share responsibility with others.

Executives have cause to wonder about time-saving promises with the advent of computers. Studies reveal that electronic data processing may actually increase the work load for the decision-maker since it speeds up the amount of information that must be digested. Furthermore, jet transportation increases the capacity for work by facilitating more travel. Since the farthest plant or subsidiary can be reached in a few hours, executives fly to these outlying areas, then spend extra time getting caught up upon returning to the office. Another affliction that has stepped-up in recent years, and that creates a source of anxiety for executives is known as the "conglomerate psychosis," the ever-present possibility that the company may merge with another—and the executive may emerge out of a job.

Wives of busy executives, faced with absentee husbands, frequently feel abandoned and resent the amount of time their husbands spend on the road and the amount their husbands usually drink; and they are fearful because of the growing number of heart attacks among the ranks of middle-aged managers and executives. Such resentment and fear cannot help but take their toll in marital discord at home. Often the wife of the hard-driving executive who is totally committed to the goals of the corporation is left wondering just how low she rates in the order of priorities that claim her husband's diffused affections.

At the opposite end of the pole from the mobile executive who is still trying to "make it" during middle age, is the man who *has* made it by middle age and suddenly has no place to go up the ladder of success. He suspects he may be a "flash in the pan." This phenomenon, called "peaking out," was touched on briefly in an earlier chapter. A business world or a society at large that confers rewards for high performance and achievement is likely to intensify "peaking-out" experiences. This form of crisis occurs in situations where a professional or career-wise person has met his goal prematurely. It is currently a prominent occupational hazard of the advertising industry. Here we find creative, imaginative geniuses—ad-men in the ad-biz—who peak out at the age of 33. The *Wall Street Journal* a year or so ago carried a big story about young men in their 20's who earn $50,000 to $75,000 a year with their clever copy in those flamboyant creative advertising agencies. And then they peak out, sometimes as early as the age of 25. When you are earning $75,000 a year at age 25 and you have arrived near the top of your profession, where do you go from there? How do you top that? What do you do for an encore? In similar plights are many others—not just in the ad-biz but in Wall Street brokerage houses and in many other professions today—including the eminent scientist who makes creative discoveries, the chemist or physicist, say, or the mathematician, who by the age of 30 has been awarded the Nobel Prize. What more can you expect from him? Peaking-out and the subsequent fear of a career dive are so tied in with our work-driven society that they become formidable when added to the crisis of middlescence.

On the current scene it is becoming more and more common to find middlescent men meeting the crisis in their careers by changing occupations. At one time it was thought that only the young, the bold, or the incompetent would consider switching careers in mid-course. But now people of all ages, and especially the middle-aged, are opting to change not just their jobs, but their whole life-styles. Not only is this pattern nationwide, but it appears in virtually every occupation. A San Francisco attorney dropped his profitable law practice and took up manufacturing shoes, while a Michigan reporter left his field to study and then to practice law. More and more clergymen are leaving their churches to go into other areas: social service, education, personnel work, counseling, politics, and so forth. A recent issue of *Life* magazine described five different Americans who had changed their careers in middle age: an Ohio salesman who became a Captain in the National Guard Eskimo Scouts in Alaska; a Chicago stockbroker who will soon have his doctorate in marine sciences; a New York insurance broker who bought a tourist type inn in Maine; a Dallas veterinarian who found he enjoyed the physical effort of unloading cargo on the dock; and a New Orleans policeman who turned to painting and now operates an open-air art gallery in the New Orleans French Quarter.

For most of these men the switch involved a drop in income and meant starting over in a new place. For all of them it meant persuading a reluctant wife to take a chance. But the change, in these cases at least, has improved the outlook and marriages of these men. Obviously a job that seemed fascinating at age 20 can lose its appeal after 20 years. In the crisis of middlescence, when the kind of work one does can aggravate other problems like alcoholism, heart attacks, worry, and divorce, these men found new challenge and new inspiration in their occupations.

No doubt the "hang loose," "do your own thing" philoso-phy of the younger generation has helped pave the way for such career-switching in mid-life. Certainly the more affluent standard of living we enjoy today enabled these men to tide over themselves and their families as they prepared for their new jobs. But the thing to note here is the fact that when men hit the crisis of middlescence they often experience a general, widespread dissatisfaction with their jobs. For every man who does switch to a more fulfilling kind of work, there are still hundreds who stick it out at the same jobs, doing something they dislike. Regardless of what response is made, the spouse and family will find it difficult to adjust unless they understand the forces at work in the man's life. The tendency to switch careers in mid-life is apparently here to stay. One writer notes that:

> More and more men are changing jobs today. Columbia University recently completed an experimental program just to help them change. There seem to be no limits to the leap; account executives have quit to become ministers, min-isters have become engineers, and engineers have turned to raising chickens. Next time you hear a man wondering whether what he's doing is what he ought to be doing, watch out. That just may be the last you'll ever see of him.[9]

The spouse of a man who decides to switch careers in middlescence must cope with her own kind of crisis in that situation. She already has her own problems, of course, with the aging process, with her unemployed-mother status, and with her own frustrations, boredom, and despair. If the couple can make their adjustment together as they take this new step they may indeed discover a closer relationship than they have ever had before—a more intimate one, be-cause they have shared deep feelings and meanings. If, on the other hand, the husband withdraws into his occupational

[9] Ann Bayer, "Beginning Again in the Middle," *Life*, June 12, 1970, p. 50.

frustration and worry, or drops out and leaves his wife to fend for herself, the spouse gap cannot help escalating at a tremendous speed.

Another form of the middlescent work crisis appears when the breadwinner finds himself out of a job. Unemployment, recession, and inflation take their toll. There is, in particular, a rising tide of unemployed managers, executives, and financial consultants who once lived high on the hog. For instance, merged corporations leave a number of executives jobless— the "merger-expendable men." Or corporations, facing a liquidity squeeze, combine certain executive positions, closing branch offices and generally cutting back. Or with cutbacks in defense expenditures, aerospace engineers and computer programmers become a glut on the market. Regardless of how it is happening, however, it is a fact that talented, highly trained men used to earning $20,000 or $30,000 a year or corporate vice-presidents accustomed to $60,000 salaries are now out of work in their middle years and unable to find immediate employment.

Often the unemployed, white-collar worker is two embarrassed to apply for unemployment benefits, finally going in for assistance after several months as a last resort. Many executives find it hard even to face the fact they have been fired. Some companies try to cushion the blow for them by using the euphemism "dis-hired," by giving them assistance in finding new employment, and by letting the ex-employee have his office and secretary for a few extra weeks. One man faked his job status for a whole summer, calling the company chauffeur to take him places and charging his telephone bills to his company credit card. One study told of the vice-president of a bank who lost his job but did not tell his family. He left every day at the same time, but instead of job-hunting he spent his day in movie theaters and in window shopping. When a bill collector finally caught up with him a few months later and repossessed the new car he had bought his son, the man told his family he had *resigned* from the bank.

Often the man who loses his job is living on anticipated income or borrowed money, like the $22,000-a-year junior executive who kept his mother in a convalescent home that cost $8,000. The pain of reckoning with a "mortgaged affluence" for financially overextended families strikes at heart and home. Furthermore, the loss of certain fringe benefits comes as a great blow—a car, expense accounts, company credit cards, free theater tickets, extravagant dinners with clients, business trips that don't have to be justified. But the crisis set in motion for these men is spiritual and psychological and economic. Many of them have assumed the company's prestige as their own, and they feel stripped of identity— like nobodies—when they lose that connection. Or they are unable to admit even to themselves that they can be replaced.

More and more groups are being formed to help unemployed professional men find jobs. One such group at the California Human Resources Office in San Francisco is called Experience Unlimited. In several metropolitan centers there is a Forty Plus Club where men help find jobs for each other. Other men rely on personal contacts, employment agencies, and management consultants (called "headhunters" in the business world).

Nearly all studies of jobless men agree that the most important thing in his life at that crisis period is an understanding, helpful wife; for here is where "for better or for worse" gets tested. The spouse may react in any number of ways, of course. She may, with him, miss the fringe benefits, finding it hard to adjust downwards in her style of living. She may be relieved, and rather enjoy the return to a simpler life and the freedom from corporate pressures. Or she may simply worry about how to explain the situation to her bridge club. In any case, there will be a noticeable drop in socializing for the unemployed executive, partly out of financial necessity, but also out of embarrassment. For many wives, the hard thing is having to uproot the family from friends and familiar surroundings.

The demands put on the marital relationship when the man is unemployed are great. It may become necessary for the wife to get a job (often at less than half what the husband made), which may be a blow to the husband's ego since he is contributing nothing to the household. One husband, whose wife went back to work as a social worker, found that working eight hours a day was certainly more interesting than taking care of the house. He had to spend a frustrating year in this situation, becoming, in essence, the family housekeeper. A psychologist addressing the problem of "the care and feeding of the jobless man" stressed several important points for the wife: she should put the family on a very tight budget, make sure her husband's clothes are taken care of for job interviews, give him encouragement and special attention, take some care in what she says concerning family problems, refrain from nagging him to do household chores while he is at home and out of work, and keep up her own morale. With such a task before her the wife has as many pressures working on her as there are on her husband!

For some couples the job loss becomes the last straw, particularly if the marriage relationship is fragile anyway, or if they are unequipped to deal with the crisis, or if one or the other spouse is unable to hang in and make things work in the light of the various middlescent difficulties. A middle-aged, former engineer reached the point of having only $24 in his pocket, $35 in the bank, and a foreclosure threat against his house. His desperate situation drove him to seek a job digging ditches for a friend in a construction firm, but he found he could not get into the union—a person had to be under 26 for that particular one. He had sent out hundreds of résumés, had a "dead file" of responses from some fifty companies. He spent days hunting work but failed even to get an interview with most companies. And, his wife and daughter have left him. We do not know to what extent this spouse tried to make things work, but evidently the couple did not have enough going for them to get them through the crisis.

Many men, after they find a job again, start reflecting on their marriage and reevaluating their spouses. Some conclude that their wives, far from being helpmates, were emotional liabilities and decide to end the marriage before another crisis causes a similar strain for them.

Of course, not all cases of job crisis end in adversity. Sometimes the corporate axe or even the much-maligned bankruptcy status can be a blessing in disguise. Consider the experience of Harold and Cathy. A reputable and successful suburban building contractor, Harold had started his own firm, building high-priced quality homes of distinction. His homes gained a well-deserved reputation for excellence in design and craftsmanship and have been featured in leading home-building journals. At the time of his business demise he employed 18 carpenters and an office staff, and maintained half a dozen trucks and a warehouse. His firm was busily engaged in constructing 25 homes that would sell in the $40,000 to $55,000 range. Suddenly, there were no buyers, as the market seemed to dry up. Meanwhile bankers, suppliers, and a whole host of creditors were clamoring for their payments. Harold had miscalculated demand and overextended commitments. He was a victim of the nationwide credit crunch and felt the painful fiscal squeeze. During the hectic period that led finally to declaration of bankruptcy, Harold and Cathy lost nearly all their "friends," who avoided them like the plague. It was a poignant experience for this couple to face their four young children and explain why there would be no Christmas presents this year—not even a tree.

Through all the financial setbacks Harold and Cathy, sentimental though it may sound, actually discovered each other anew as they closed ranks and deepened their love for each other. The family made plans for a new life; they sold their expensive home—about the only thing they had left—and moved into an old, rundown shack in the countryside, which Harold completely remodeled into a charming, rustic home. They altered their entire life-style from affluence to a simpler arrangement and found they enjoyed it more. They were relieved to be removed from the competitive life of a busy building contractor. Harold became a free-lance photographer, turning an early hobby into a vocation, and he finds his new work enjoyable and fulfilling. Ironic as it may seem, the couple are now grateful for the experience of bankruptcy, for they doubt whether they, without going through the fiscal fires, would have discovered their newfound vocational and marital happiness.

As they must make the adjustments required when the children leave home, the couple must face themselves, each other, and their marriage in relation to problems involving the career at middle age. The middlescent malaise is bound to heighten the usual tensions and pressures associated with the job. Add to that the real uncertainty about having a job at all, or the fear that a person will never find any satisfaction in his work, and there is a crisis fanning the flames of the ever-burning spouse gap.

GALLOPING GAPOSIS AND THE ALLURE OF ADULTERY

The storm of middlescence has hit with a frenzy and the marriage is fraught with crises that are blowing the spouses farther and farther apart. As we survey the revolution this creates on the homefront, it becomes apparent that many of the "new" difficulties are not entirely new at all, but rooted in old, unresolved conflicts and problems which have resurfaced. For instance, the woman who is overly dependent on her children after they have left home usually has always found it difficult to value herself as a whole, individual person. And the man who is unable to adjust to changes in job responsibilities probably has always doubted his capabilities.

Middle age, then, intensifies all the difficulties we thought would go away some day—either in our own behavior or that of our spouse. But there they are, waiting for us at mid-life, bigger than ever. Sometimes the crisis problem is a more intense repetition or variation of a problem we've always lived with. But now the spouse can no longer stand it and no longer expects it to go away. A sense of frustration and of time fleeting finally stirs a person to act. This search for help may lead to relief from the old tension—to real growth and change—or it may come too late.

One counselor tells of a woman who threw temper tantrums like a child, even in early marriage. Furthermore, she intensely disliked having company. Her husband, on the other hand, enjoyed entertaining people at home but his wife's tantrums usually made things go her way. He was able to tolerate this situation for many years, but finally decided he no longer *had* to put up with her childish antics. By the time they sought help he had lost interest in his wife and had found someone else, so he did not try to recoup his marriage.

Another case involved a husband who felt very subservient to his father, for whom he worked, and who seemed unable to communicate with his wife. Very early in their marriage he fell into the habit of stopping off for drinks with the boys after work. After more than fifteen years his wife finally found she could not fight their marital situation alone—he literally was uncommunicative with her. They were facing grave financial problems because his father was not paying him enough to meet their household expenses, and his drinking was getting steadily worse. Her consideration of divorce finally precipitated the crisis which brought them to a marriage counselor.

Yet another illustration of the "old problem/new crisis" syndrome is the husband who constantly had extramarital affairs throughout his years of marriage. His wife knew about them but kept hoping he would change. Finally she threatened to leave him unless he got some help. In therapy it was discovered that the man was much more dependent upon his wife than he realized—which was a carryover from his dependence on his mother. His flirtations were his way of escaping that dependence by letting him play the role of the strong man to weak women.

So it is that the early gaps in the marriage-go-round, swept aside in the routine of marriage, finally assert themselves again in the throes of middle age. Feeling that the marriage does not provide an adequate sense of personal identity and significance, one or the other partner, or both together, will often go from apathy to some kind of action, emotionally powerful if not physically violent. "For," as Rollo May notes, "no human being can stand the perpetually numbing experience of his own powerlessness." [10] Attempts to assert one's power can take any number of forms: acute illness, surrender to acting old before one is; belittling, badgering, and baiting the spouse in continual bickering (in the manner of Edward Albee's characters in *Who's Afraid of Virginia Woolf?*) ; alcoholism; adultery. The misunderstandings pyramid while the gaps become increasingly difficult to bridge. Each spouse, convinced of the righteousness of his own action, passes a point of no return and speeds on to a galloping gaposis.

Two primary manifestations of responses to the growing gap can be seen in the retreat into excessive drinking and in the advance into extramarital affairs. The prevalence of these two activities was noted by a Michigan judge reporting on his experience with divorce cases. The reasons people began divorce proceedings after being married 25 to 30 years, the judge concluded, could be summarized as either a new love interest or an old drinking problem. Behind the drinking and the infidelity are, no doubt, the more general problems

[10] May, *Love and Will*, p. 14.

of lack of communication and intimacy, and/or boredom in the marital relationship. The alcohol and the affair become the triggering points for the trouble. For instance, a woman sued her husband for divorce, charging him with adultery as the primary cause. In fact, however, their marriage was already on the rocks and the "other woman" was used by both partners as a weapon in their battle against each other, and as an object for their many grievances. The husband felt powerless in the marriage and the affair was his way to assert himself. The wife felt powerless in their marriage and her husband's affair became the occasion for her to assert herself. Similar cases can be cited in regard to the pattern of alcoholism.

In the case of alcoholism the individual turns inward to a solitary diversion and solace. In the case of infidelity there is a reaching out for another person's warmth and sympathy. Which direction a person chooses probably depends largely on his own personality makeup and experience. But certainly both are reactions to problems which have intensified in the period of middlescence as the nest empties and the business world teeters, and both contribute in their own ways to the spouse gap escalation.

Taken as a whole, alcoholism climbs a steep 50 percent in the 40-to-60 age group over those in their 30's. In this period of stress and tension when the individual is restless, sleepless, and irritable, alcohol may be resorted to for support and relaxation. In terms of marital problems, however, alcohol provides a release of control over pent-up feelings of hostility. At the extreme, the drunken spouse may become physically violent as well as irrational and unreasonable. Over the years, of course, excessive drinking can do the individual himself great harm, bodily and psychically. Even if the drinking does not go to an extreme, the lack of control it brings can cause estrangement. Here the following observation is most pertinent:

Many know from first-hand experience the drunken remark that cuts to the core. Later you listen to the apology and the plea to be forgiven for hurting your feelings. What makes you uncomfortable is that the remark hit so deep and was so painfully astute that you keep wondering just how drunk the speaker really was. Alcohol releases inhibitions, and a great deal of immaturity lies just below the surface, held there by our ability to suppress the child in every man. The social drinking which is so common in our society has this rather unexpected side effect of becoming a serious source of marital conflict by opening up the Pandora's box of childhood.[11]

Such verbal (and sometimes physical) wounding, while direct and personal, is not what we mean by honest and openness in communication!

But of all the responses a man or woman may make to the complications of the middlescent malaise, the most tempting is probably the extramarital affair. Against the drabness of the old marriage the allure of adultery beckons with the promise of excitement and pleasure. Frequently this may take the form of the office romance, where propinquity, opportunity, and shared experience create a congenial atmosphere. Or the husband may meet a woman with whom he can talk about things he no longer dares to tell his wife. Or the wife may find herself with a friend who offers a sympathetic ear and an understanding heart. Conversation about marriage disappointments gives way to enjoyment of the new companionship, and it becomes an easy slide from there into sexual relations.

The point is, when a person is unhappy, someone is always handy, who is also either unhappy or very much available to bring happiness to him or her in this particular way. Therefore, the temptation is great for spouses having marital problems to have extramarital consolations. Some people do

[11] McCready, *Our Bed Is Flourishing*, p. 147.

find solace in these relationships, which tends to make them more frustrated and disappointed with their marriages. On the other hand, if there has been little more than physical attachment in the liaison, the partner may be brought back to a frame of mind where he wants to give his marital relationship another whirl.

Whether or not a dissatisfied spouse is unfaithful depends largely on his or her individual makeup and attitude toward marriage. Some people carry on outside affairs with little or no provocation from the partner whereas others would never stray, whatever the provocation and temptation. But more often than not, under the right conditions, a desire for extramarital relations will overcome the usual control. This is especially true when the circumstances are such that a spouse feels deprived and unloved at home, or suffers a career setback and needs reassurance, or experiences the impact of middle age in terms of diminishing sexual attraction. He or she then reaches out for a new paramour to fill the void and finds there is a responding "other person." The same man or woman might never have become unfaithful if everything had continued to run smoothly and well and remained unchanging.

Among other things, too, one must have the means for conducting the affairs: infidelity is sometimes expensive and time-consuming!

There are some people who are able both to maintain a stable marriage, and to indulge in extramarital affairs with apparent ease. Usually they find in each relationship something that is lacking in the other and they feel that the two styles of life enhance each other. One man reflected on an experience in which he made love to his mistress, Mary, and then went home to make love to his wife, Laurie:

> But how could I enjoy it so much—and yet want Mary all the more? Had a most unoriginal thought: Perhaps a man need not love only one woman and in only one way. Laurie

157

the wife, old friend, home base; Mary the lost half of me, a grand passion, dream of love come true. Perhaps I could love each in a special way; perhaps that was the simple, obvious, and overlooked answer.[12]

Another man felt his outside affairs kept him feeling younger, eager, and interested in life. In many ways this arrangement of having a wife and marriage for home and family, but also mistresses and affairs for spice and excitement in sexual variety apes a practice carried on in other cultures. Infidelity in other traditions may not be considered wrong, but is regarded as a normal human desire for newness.

A recent book, *The Sexual Behavior of the Married Man in France* indicates that the 1,000 husbands interviewed, all who had been married 20 years or longer had felt the sexual fire gradually go out of their marriages but saw no reason for divorce because of extramarital affairs outside the home. Most of them considered love and physical desire to be opposites: a man loves and stays with his wife, while finding erotic pleasure and satisfaction with his mistresses. No doubt the conventions of society—in this case, an acceptance of the practice of sexual variety—have an influence on the behavior of Frenchmen. In American society we find a curious paradox: general disapproval of adultery, even among those who have had affairs, while the practice itself appears to be growing.

One can doubtless point to situations where a mature, emotionally stable person has an affair with someone else which grows out of genuine respect and affection, and which does not harm the marital relationship itself. On this point authors Levy and Munroe offer this comment:

Sometimes this procedure works very well. I suspect, however, that it works well only in those marriages which are fundamentally sound anyway. A man who is genuinely fond

[12] Hunt, *The Affair,* p. 98.

of his wife, thoroughly responsible as a husband, and well integrated as a personality can handle hidden deviations from monogamy adequately. If the marriage is already disturbed, however, or if the man is himself very much upset by his behaviour, the results of concealment are often as unhappy as they are unexpected.[13]

While it is interesting to note that there are rare couples who have worked out a relationship so satisfactory that it allows for other intimate relationships without major disruption, it is not our primary concern to discover how this is done. Here we are looking at the marriage which *is* disturbed and for which the affair represents a crisis.

Thus it is that most affairs arising out of the middle-age malaise rarely are undertaken in the name of love. In many cases, the romantic infatuation is an impossibly neurotic one —that is, the other person is unsuitable as a potential partner, or is cruel or a source of great guilt. Edmund Bergler contends that the middle-aged rebel deliberately moves toward an impossible situation because he wants to fail and to suffer in the affair. And, since misery loves company, that is exactly what happens.

Those people who want the extramarital affair to be one in which intimacy is limited to occasional meetings and sexual relations do not usually grow closer after their initial consummation. Their pleasure and gratification comes from keeping things more or less superficial. The affair may eventually die out without having breached the marriages of the two parties. Or a major crisis may occur, if one or the other party in the liaison decides to go deeper into the relationship, or if the spouse of one or the other finds out and demands a showdown.

If the unfaithful party is one who believes every relationship must be complete and totally committed, then the affair usually does provoke a disruptive crisis in the life of his or

<hr />

[13] Levy and Munroe, *The Happy Family,* pp. 95-96.

her marriage. Often the situation calls for resolution one way or the other, since the person's conscience may not let him give himself to two people at the same time. This dilemma then becomes a terrible struggle between two ways of life; the new love and the promise of emotional intensity, renewed youthfulness, and realization of happiness; or the old spouse, with shared experiences, family ties and personal identity.

Of course there is no end to the rationalizations that human beings can dredge up to justify doing what is really wanted. Under the guise of making an effort to save his marriage, the person desiring to go with the new partner may effectively hasten the disintegration of his marriage.

> He believes that he is thinking things through in hopes of finding the reasons for his marital discontent; actually, he is juggling the books of married life in order to find his new love superior at every point. He means to talk things out with his spouse in order to clear up their misunderstandings and differences; actually the discussions give him the chance to be openly angry and hostile, and to find any similar anger or hostility on his mate's part a proof of the hopelessness of the situation. He tries to damp down conflict between them by truces or avoidance, but only succeeds in starving the relationship to death.[14]

Although the presence of spouse and family cannot hold a person who has really determined to end the marriage, their presence can continue to be a constraint toward faithfulness in marriage. Every encounter of an illicit nature runs the risk of harm to one's mate, the children, the marriage. This is why a marriage which goes on the rocks after the children are grown and gone from home exerts less control over extramarital desires and their fulfillment.

How the spouse handles the discovery of an affair can make a great difference in whether the crisis leads to divorce. An attack by the wronged person may lead the other to be-

[14] Hunt, *The Affair,* p. 187.

come defensive and draw him or her deeper in the direction of the third party in the triangle. This is paricularly true if many old resentments and hostilities have been stored up in the marital relationship. The new person has no ax to grind, has no old problems to be settled, and offers the allure of romance and comfort. At least one wife, however, was objective and sensitive enough to react in a way which brought her erring husband back:

> "I'll never forget," says Jim, "how Alice behaved when my sordid little affair with the girl at the office blew up in her face. I knew it must be hurting her terribly—but she didn't whine and she didn't lash out. She sat me down, looked me straight in the eyes, and asked me where she had gone wrong and what this girl had that she hadn't. In that moment I knew what a fine person Alice really was, and I felt ashamed of the whole business. From that moment the other girl didn't have a chance." [15]

Among other things, Alice could view her husband's indiscretion on its own terms, not in the light of an absolute, categorical judgment that says infidelity is evil. Too often a principle about affairs is imposed with no attempt to understand the reason behind it, and the marriage is doomed. Or if the partner does forgive the spouse, he or she may never forget the incident or let the other forget it and the marriage continues to deteriorate anyway.

Act Two has taken us through the complications of the middlescent malaise, the suspense of the sexual readjustment at mid-life, and into the crisis of the escalating spouse gap. The children are grown and on their own, the job offers little sense of personal fulfillment, and the atmosphere is charged with the temptation to seek comfort in illicit sex. The curtain thus falls on the marriage drama with the crisis in full sway. We are ready to explore the climax in Act Three.

[15] Mace, *Success in Marriage,* p. 100.

VI

CLIMAX: WEDLOCK BECOMES DEADLOCK

Which way will the marriage go? Can the couple weather the storms that shake their vows? Many middlescent marriages today stand on this threshold of climax. What kind of resolution is possible as we imagine marriage as it might be?

Before setting our imaginations to work, however, we need to look at some of the last steps in the process leading to the climax of our marriage drama. Basically we find an intensification of the old problem of blocked or closed or nonexistent communication. That is to say, wedlock becomes deadlock when there is no attempt to work out differences in a constructive fashion, whether by stubborn refusal to do so or through pathetic resignation that change is impossible or out of blind inability to see that something is wrong.

A clash of personalities can mean an opportunity for achieving greater insight into oneself, appreciation for the other, and mutual understanding together. But for these things to happen the lines of communication must be open. More often than not when there is conflict we reinforce its destructive potential by blocking the flow of communication —at least verbally. However, our dissatisfactions, annoyances, angers, and frustrations continue to be expressed nonverbally, and our behavior becomes our meaning—or the going becomes the goal.

THE MEDIUM IS THE MESSAGE

Everyone knows that communication is a complex process. One of the prevailing fallacies is our assumption that all communication is verbal and, therefore, if we don't talk, we can avoid the distress and conflict that come when we express ourselves. Actually, however, the nonverbal level of communication is very real, is hard to disguise, and has a profound effect on all parties involved. This is how one study describes the process:

> The family is an interacting communications network in which every member from the day-old baby to the seventy-year-old grandmother influences the nature of the entire system and in turn is influenced by it. . . . The system tends, by nature, to keep itself in balance. An unusual action by one member invariably results in a compensating reaction by another member. If mother hates to take Sunday drives but hides this feeling from her husband, the message is nevertheless somehow broadcast throughout the family communications network, and it may be Johnny, the four-year-old, who becomes "carsick" and ruins the Sunday drive.[1]

In this light consider the husband who says to his wife, "Yes, dear, I want to go to the movie with you," but as he speaks he is looking through the mail, loosening his tie, avoiding the door, and inching toward his favorite chair. The point is, a marriage is a feeling system in which the behavior and attitudes of one partner has an effect on the other, whether it is verbalized or not. Even silence is communication. One man simply could not believe that his wife had left him. "Why," he said, "we never had an argument in the 16 years we were married, and I came home one night to find her gone!"

Just as all kinds of negative feelings get transmitted by nonverbal behavior, so also a couple may use their verbiage to cover up feelings of tenderness and warmth. In this case, if the partners can become aware of the truth of their nonverbal impulses they can use that behavior to get in touch with their real feelings. Often patterns get established over

[1] Lederer and Jackson, *Mirages of Marriage,* p. 14.

the years that are almost impossible to break down. One of the founding leaders of Esalen Institute in California, William Schutz, described a group session in which a man and woman were mutually critical, angrily attacking and counterattacking each other. When asked to stop talking but to continue communicating, they put their arms around each other in a long and warm embrace. Everyone was surprised, including the man and woman who had been locked in combat.

As the group later discussed the above incident, it became clear that these two people felt real affection for each other, but each was afraid the other did not feel the same way. Dr. Schutz goes on with the following detailed description:

> The woman felt that he didn't like her and she was very angry and bitter about this and took every opportunity to get even. When their real feelings came through, the need for the attack and defense was eliminated. They did, in fact, like each other, the sharpness disappeared, and they began building a closer, more supportive relationship. Here the verbalizing was not just obscuring the issue as in the first example, but it was conveying the very opposite of the true situation. The behavior was hostility but the underlying feeling was affection along with fear.[2]

While this couple was not married, their verbal/nonverbal dichotomy is indicative of the kind that occurs in marriage as patterns become more and more rigid over the years. In this case the real message is not the one being sent, and misunderstanding is greatly escalated.

Messages, both verbal and nonverbal, can conflict with each other, with the intention of the sender, and with the interpretation of the receiver. Often the message sent is not the one received—and this is true of behavior as well as words. It is estimated that spouses miscommunicate 20 per-

[2] William C. Schutz, *Joy* (New York: Grove Press, 1967) , p. 139.

cent of the time, and that this faulty transaction wrecks marriages that might otherwise be workable.

Almost all the respondents in our Marriage Interview Schedule said they would like to be honest with their spouses and vice versa. In conversations, however, many people have admitted that lack of honest communication was a major problem. With such value placed on honesty, why is it so hard to achieve and maintain over the years?

For one thing, when couples reach middle age they are often afraid to be honest, especially if they have not had a pattern of open communication all along. They have no idea how the other person feels and thinks about their relationship and how his feelings have changed. They are afraid to blurt out how they feel and risk endangering their marriage. Perhaps one partner regards honesty as aggression and controls such expression as an undesirable impulse. Perhaps one partner refuses to let honesty flow as a two-way street, preferring to dish it out but not to receive it. We can identify various people, including ourselves, with such communication troublemakers as "The Hot Retort," "The Cold Sulk," "The Deep Freeze," "The Wounded Martyr," "The Righteous One." [3] Trust depends on open and truthful communication between both spouses and on consistency between verbal and nonverbal behavior. When such communication is clear, change and growth can be understood, adjusted to, and/or commented upon as the relationship evolves.

While simply letting fly, willy-nilly, with how you feel can break up the marriage, lack of engagement on matters that eat away at the relationship can eventually tear it down. A couple must achieve a balance between the two extremes. To this end George Bach and Peter Wyden have devoted their book *The Intimate Enemy* to training couples in how to fight fair in love and marriage. Acknowledging that it is good and

[3] Rodenmayer, *I John Take Thee Mary.*

165

healthy to fight (verbally) in marriage, the authors stress the importance of fighting fairly. Untrained fighters, under pressure, are tempted to strike at weak points, to throw in irrelevancies, to horde grievances (called "gunny-sacking"), and then let fly for the kill over some minor incident. The authors explain their purpose as follows:

> When our trainees fight according to our flexible system of rules, they find that the natural tensions and frustrations of two people living together can be greatly reduced. Since they live with fewer lies and inhibitions and have discarded outmoded notions of etiquette, these couples are free to grow emotionally, to become more productive and more creative, as individuals in their own right and also as pairs. Their sex lives tend to improve. . . . Their communications improve and, as a result, they face fewer unpleasant surprises from their partners. . . . They feel less vulnerable and more loving toward each other because they are protected by an umbrella of reasonable standards for what is fair and foul in their relationship. Perhaps best of all, they are liberated to be themselves.[4]

Such an understanding of the nature of intimate fighting is implicit in the story of the couple celebrating their fiftieth wedding anniversary. Reporters gathered around them, asking how they met, what kind of life they had together, and so on. When asked if they ever fought, both acknowledged they did. Then one reporter asked the wife whether she had ever considered getting a divorce in those fifty years. Surprised, she answered, "Why, no!" Then with a glint in her eye she added, "Murder, yes—but divorce? Never!" Bach and Wyden have discovered in their training program that their graduates attain a level of honesty and expression in their fighting that is noisier and more intense than in most relationships, but creates intimacy which makes them less susceptible to either boredom or divorce.

[4] Bach and Wyden, *The Intimate Enemy,* pp. 1-2.

166

Not all couples make the effort to iron out the differences between them. Perhaps one or the other partner is simply apathetic. There are men and women who passively try to sit out their troubles—or sleep, eat, or drink them away—or who forget them by watching TV, going to movies, playing golf or bridge, or any number of other games. They seem unable to do the one thing they need most, attack the problem directly. Eventually, of course, the negative feelings either explode like a volcano or are suppressed into dormant nonfeeling. Rollo May writes that the chief block to therapy for many patients is an inability to feel. They have attained an evenness in living and thinking which gives them the sense that nothing really matters. In this regard May writes:

> Apathy is particularly important because of its close relation to love and will. Hate is not the opposite of love; apathy is. The opposite of will is not indecision—which actually may represent the struggle of the effort to decide, as in William James—but being uninvolved, detached, unrelated to the significant events. The issue of will never can arise.[5]

The apathetic person needs to be led to the place where he can feel again; and unless he learns to recognize anger and hostility he will be unable to recognize love and affection.

In many instances it seems easier for the woman to express feelings and emotions than for the man to do so. David Mace traces this difference to cultural conditioning, in which we expect girls to cry and be emotional and talk a lot while encouraging boys to keep a stiff upper lip and act like a man (i.e., show no softness, emotion, or hurt) and expressing admiration for the strong, silent type. Yet women long for men to be more gentle, more open, and more intimate, and many of them trace their marital conflicts to this problem. Perhaps, Dr. Mace suggests, men long to be more expressive too. "The

[5] May, *Love and Will*, p. 29.

strange truth is that when a man has to retreat into silence before his wife, he experiences a sense of deep disappointment. This is in fact the last thing he wants to do." [6] The author enjoins the wife of the silent husband to do all she can to draw him out of his abyss, in the assurance that what he most longs for is a relationship where he can be himself and can express his pent-up feelings freely and honestly.

There is perhaps no greater way to widen the spouse gap than for one or the other mate to bottle up his feelings and thoughts and problems and shut the other out.

But sometimes, too, the communication problem arises because one or the other person has no awareness of what he or she is doing. Each may feel he is trying to make the marriage work, and assume that trouble comes from the way the spouse handles things. For instance, what one regards as love may be a suffocating prison to the other. Consider the wife who "loves" her husband so much she calls him three or four times a day at the office, wants to know where he is every minute, and worries him to distraction when they are separated. Or the husband who "loves" his wife so much he surprises her with gifts he has chosen without her consultation— things which she must use, however, like a car, a washing machine, a vacuum cleaner, or a house.

Such misunderstandings cannot but cause great heartache in the marriage. "The person who is seeking the perfect love and attempting to achieve it by being sweet, thoughtful, and giving, usually ends up feeling used. The person who is looking for a helpmate in his quest for success is not giving love, but is expecting his spouse to accept status and achievement as reward enough for her efforts." [7] Unless the couple can communicate their differences as differences and not as superior/inferior judgments or as good/bad modes of behavior, they will never reach a mutually satisfactory relationship.

[6] Mace, *Success in Marriage,* p. 88.
[7] Lederer and Jackson, *Mirages of Marriage,* p. 175.

Wedlock becomes deadlock, and the spouses play out their roles in resignation or rebellion.

CELLMATES, CHECKMATES, ROOMMATES, STALEMATES

The patterns of interaction developed in marriages are, of course, many and varied. Our interviews have revealed at least four types of middle-aged marriages which can be described as having arrived at a climax point of deadlock. We call these forms of the mating game Cellmates, Checkmates, Roommates, and Stalemates.

We invite you to consider whether or not you and your spouse have entered into a variation of one of the mating games described in these four portraits. If your marriage is troubled, we hope you will face it like it is, and then imagine it like it might be if pressed to the kind of deadlock these situations exemplify.

Cellmates

Howard and Rosie have been married for twenty years, but both confess that their marriage is meaningless. Both reason, however, that since they have been together this long, they might just as well stick it out. At least they know what to expect from one another and have made peace with their situation. Their marriage is one of endurance. They are virtually imprisoned cellmates.

Besides, they feel that their situation leaves them little choice. Howard is pastor of a conservative Lutheran church and thinks that his congregation would be shocked if they suspected that all is not well in the parsonage. Surely they would not condone a divorce. Howard presumes it would mean his leaving the ministry if he and his wife ever separated.

Rosie does not really care what the church would think, since she never really wanted Howard to become a clergyman in the first place. It was his idea. When they were first married, Howard worked as a purchasing agent for a nationwide department store. Then suddenly he got fed up with the business world in general and his own job in particular. At the same time he became vitally interested in religion and at the suggestion of his pastor enrolled in seminary and was ordained upon graduation. Rosie felt her whole life-style was being altered. She had already set her mind on future expectations—which did not include being a minister's wife. She resented Howard's decision, yet has felt obligated to go along. Consequently, she participates as little as possible in church affairs, but just enough to be noticed.

Rosie prefers to turn her efforts toward her own world of art and music, and is an accomplished pianist. She has decided to have a life of her own in which she can find satisfaction. She takes music lessons from a highly gifted concert pianist and, in turn, gives private instruction to six or eight advanced pupils. At the same time, however, she is fearful about her ability to support herself entirely without Howard, so she has no plans to leave him.

Howard always has a ready excuse for Rosie's absence at important church functions; usually he explains that her migraine headache is acting up again. Apart from the embarrassment of always having to make excuses for his wife's less-than-enthusiastic response to church activities, Howard is not too bothered by the marital relationship. Both he and Rosie are resigned to being cellmates, locked into their "morbidity marriage," condemned to each other for the rest of their lives.

Checkmates

Gloria and Peter have two teen-age children, a boy and a girl. Their marriage seems held together by a constant contest of wills in which each antagonizes the other. Yet there is also a deep, affectionate bond, and nearly every quarrel is followed by torrid lovemaking, during which Gloria experiences an entire series of orgasms and Peter is totally spent.

Both are strong willed and reluctant to give in or compromise. Each, it seems, is out to score debating points on the other. They argue over everything. The name of their game is one-upmanship.

For the most part, however, their incessant arguments are over trifling matters. If he accuses her of not being a good mother, she charges that he is a lousy provider, "a penny-pinching miser." If he nags her to balance the checkbook stubs, she purposely lets it go until their checks start bouncing. If he gives the son a bad time, she is likely to pick on the daughter. Once they were all dressed up to go out for dinner, when, at the last minute, Gloria refused to leave the house and Peter went without her.

Another time, at a party, Peter, after a few drinks, became extremely friendly with one of the women guests. Gloria, watching from across the room, countered by allowing a male friend all kinds of liberties. When they returned home, accusations and countercharges flew with fury. After the shouting died down, however, the couple enjoyed their usual lovemaking.

Gloria's and Peter's arguments are the talk of the neighborhood. Several times the neighbors have called in the police to quiet things down when noise from the shouting and bickering became excessive.

The battling couple have thought of splitting up. At one time they went as far as dividing up community property so that both ends of the living room looked like a garage sale. But thus far they have always been able to call a truce and then celebrate the ending of hostilities.

Outside observers may think that Gloria's and Peter's marriage is ripping apart at the seams. Yet they are bound closely together in their "lover's quarrel." Theirs is a checkmate relationship. Locked in combat, their marriage amounts to a competitive arms race. Unable to live with or without each other, Gloria and Peter have learned to hurt each other with finesse, and each seems to find his greatest pleasure (outside the physical pleasure in the bedroom) in seeing the other one fail. In their game of one-upmanship, however, both are held in checkmate, with neither one winning or losing.

Roommates

Bill and Donna have a marriage of convenience characterized by little more than simply living together in the same split-level, suburban house. They are fairly formal and cool with one another. However, their relationship was not always this distant.

During a long, three-year engagement period while Bill was finishing medical school, the two were accomplished lovers and indulged their passions frequently. The early years of marriage were also characterized by coital activity four or five times a week. Now, however, their sex life together is virtually dormant, since Bill is "turned off" about sex.

The big change came when Bill discovered that Donna was keeping company with other men. He suddenly lost interest in sex and threw himself ever more intensively into his medical practice as a gynecologist. Bill is vaguely aware of the fact that Donna is satisfying her sex needs elsewhere and doesn't seem to mind.

Bill and Donna have developed a tolerable division of labor: she keeps house, cooks the meals, provides him with clean shirts and socks, and he "brings home the bacon" in ample supply. They have both agreed to care for and nurture their four children as best they can.

Donna says now that none of her early affairs were serious and feels she would have stopped them if Bill had put his foot down about them and thereby demonstrated his love for her. As it is, she has ceased to care what he thinks. Lately she has been considering going to business school as insurance against a time when she might possibly have to support herself. In the meantime, she finds the limited satisfaction

172

of being a mother and a doctor's wife preferable to the uncertainty of any other life.

Bill and Donna have not openly said so, but one suspects that when the children grow up and become independent Bill and Donna will end their marriage of convenience as roommates and seek more satisfying relationships.

Stalemates

Jean's and Walter's marriage cannot really be described as a very vital one. In fact, it's downright dull and tedious. Walter is forty-five and drives a bakery truck six days a week on his own delivery route. He is dog-tired when he comes home from work. Nearly every night after dinner he plops in front of the TV set and watches one program after another until he dozes off to sleep.

Jean wakes him up after awhile. Then it's off to bed they go for a night's sleep, to be followed by the same repetitive work-eat-TV-sleep routine, day in and day out. Intercourse is strictly a once-a-week, Saturday-night affair, with few preliminaries. The couple have no children and they rarely go out. Apathy and inertia characterize their life and their marriage, which is getting staler by the hour.

The only time there is any spark in the household is during the hunting season. Walter perks up and breaks his lethargy to go duck hunting and deer hunting, carefully packing his gear for trips into the hunting country. This activity he does with two or three other buddies, who are also bakery truck drivers—but never with Jean accompanying them.

Jean spends all her time puttering around the house and garden. She and Walter do not talk much together and seem to have little to talk about. Through the years they have not developed new interests, with each taking the other one pretty much for granted. Lately, however, Jean has come to feel that something is missing in their marriage. She has begun to discuss her dissatisfaction with the family doctor, whom she is visiting because of her general feeling of fatigue and a recent spell of muscle spasms.

It frightens Jean somewhat to think of rocking her marriage boat, since she has so little self-esteem. For the most part, neither Jean nor Walter dares comment on the other's behavior or the nature of their marriage. Each is afraid of what the other might do or say in response to criticism. All is forgiveness and unrequested succor—and boredom and apathy and stale air. Both Walter and Jean are caught in a lockstep —stalemated. In their marriage they are like two robots going through the motions of life in a habitual, lifeless pattern.

There are other forms of the mating game, but these will serve as examples of the deadlock which can arise when genuine communication is lost in marriage. From this deadlock the relationship may move to a plain loss of interest and further disintegration, in which continuing even the pretext of a marriage is not worth the effort. Or the situation may give rise to unexpected and bizarre behavior on the part of one of the spouses.

THE SPECTER OF DIVORCE

If in reality or in your imagination you have reached the final climax of a deadlocked marriage, there are three possible ways to approach the gap. One way is to live in one of the patterns described in the previous sections as variations of the mating game. Another, providing both you and your spouse want to make things work and are willing to risk change, is to find some ways to bridge the gap, and this alternative is the subject of the next and last chaper. Or, a third and last resort is to carry through with divorce, dissolve the union, and build a new life from there.

Before jumping to this last decision, the individuals or the couple together could well seek some counseling help prior to visiting their lawyers. Too often divorce is not a solution to the personality difficulties that created the interpersonal problem. The mate can be divorced but the neurosis can't, and the person may just continue having the same trouble over and over. Or, if the dissatisfaction with the marriage is tied up with the pressing problems of middle age, then weathering that storm and preserving the marriage ship can be more rewarding in the long run than changing vessels or heading for a new port. This is not to say that a couple should never resort to divorce. One doctor makes this comment:

> It is said that divorce brings out the worst in people. No doubt it is often the best solution and the only solution. Couples who are destroying each other sometimes do divorce and make good second marriages. And in many an instance it is clear that no marriage is far better than a bad marriage; for a bad marriage can breed hatred and can destroy both body and soul. But the process of separation is apt to be nasty.[8]

Under a number of circumstances divorce may be the only real alternative, but it is well to consider the other possible solutions first. If neither partner is able to function with the other without serious physical or emotional pain, it is likely the time has come for separation.

While marriage may be difficult, divorce, however, is difficult too. The major problem for divorced persons is often sheer loneliness. For instance, it has been established that among Caucasians those who have been divorced have the highest suicide rate. Separation and divorce, for the husband usually mean leaving his home and finding other living quarters. He suddenly finds himself having to cope with everyday problems like washing and mending his clothes. For the wife, the absence of the spouse leaves a void, no matter how bad their relationship has been. She now has no one to cook or clean or sew for. As time passes, the divorced person has the

[8] Saul, *Fidelity and Infidelity*, p. 83.

problem of trying to find someone for companionship. A divorced woman writes:

"No, I don't miss him—but I do miss having *someone*. And there is no one. Where does one look, at my age, for intelligence, humor, and compassion? Not where I used to look. And I don't know where else to go instead. I believe I have grown immensely. I feel capable of a loving, loyal, dependable relationship—and yet I have not even dated in months! There *must* be someone. I can only wait and hope." [9]

At this point it is interesting to note that only a fairly small percentage of those whose marriage broke up because of an affair actually married the other person. In his study for *The Affair*, Morton Hunt discovered that only about one-tenth of his interviewees had married, or were planning to marry, the person with whom he or she had an affair. While a third of the people were divorced as a result of such affairs, only half of them actually carried through and married the other person. Whereas the romance may have thrived in relation to the intolerable marriage, the dissolution of the marriage forces the spouse and new partner into a new intimacy which causes a new strain. One woman and man who did marry each other had trouble shortly after their wedding and then broke up. His periods of silent withdrawal led her to doubt the validity of his accusations about his first wife and to think that maybe he had shut her out rather than vice versa, as he had said.

As we have pointed out before, the gaposis in marriage is rarely a sudden phenomenon. Rather, there is a gradual disintegration of the relationship, or a gradual realization by the spouses that they did not have enough in common in the first place. A man discovers that his interests have broadened while his wife's have not. A woman realizes after her children are grown and gone that she and her husband never had anything in common except sex. The difference in their value

[9] Hunt, *The Affair*, p. 253.

systems was exemplified in the fact that she loved nature—flowers, bird-watching, bicycling, conservation causes—while he liked to hunt, fish, and go duck shooting.

So the marriage falls apart when there is no longer enough to hold it together and some event brings home that disclosure. The event may be huge, some scandalous affair, or it may be small, as in the case of the woman who was liberated by losing weight! Joan and Phil never had had much in common, were not sexually adjusted, and communicated very little. Joan felt that their situation simply had to be this way and turned her attention to raising their two children. But everyone nagged her to lose weight, and after she did she suddenly realized she was attractive and desirable to other men. With that change she became aware that she could make other changes in her life, and she told Phil she wanted a divorce. They visited marriage counselors but to no avail as her mind was already made up.

Even when divorce is agreed upon as the best solution, the actual breakup, for a couple in middle age especially, is usually a traumatic experience. "Euphoria and depression often coexist in the same person. If separation is a kind of dying, death involves mourning and melancholia. No matter how miserable a marriage may have been, divorce is a terrible defeat." [10] When this failure to make it in marriage hits home, the person may experience damage to his self-esteem as well as guilt, grief, resentment, self-pity, and depression. The marriage crisis becomes a life crisis.

This is what happened to Maureen. She and Al married, after a short courtship, on the basis of a strong physical attraction. He was twenty-one and she was twenty. From the beginning they shared few interests, with little to bind them together except their three children. Al made fun of Maureen's love of reading, music, and church interest. Maureen despised Al's silences, his crudities, and his demand-

[10] Richard L. Rubenstein, *Morality and Eros* (New York: McGraw-Hill Book Co., 1970), p. 141.

ing ways. But they made a life together—less for better than for worse. Then after twenty years Al came home and suggested a divorce. Maureen took the news calmly, knowing they really had no marriage between them anyway. There were no big scenes, no accusations, no crying, and a month later Maureen flew to Mexico for the decree.

Upon her return the impact hit her. She had to learn how to handle financial responsibilities—getting along on alimony and support money for their two younger children. But more important she withdrew into herself, ignoring even the few invitations that came from friends. She felt vague aches and pains, a consuming tiredness. She cried a good deal of the time. Then one day Maureen heard her daughter talking on the phone to her friends and it jarred her out of her self-pity. She suddenly felt furious with herself and set out to make a life with the many good years before her. She joined clubs, started entertaining, got a part-time job, lost weight, bought some new clothes, started her music again. It was not easy, but Maureen lived past her crisis.

Kenneth and Irene Donelson, in their book *Married Today, Single Tomorrow: Marriage Breakup and the Law,* encourage divorced people to do something about their depressions: sleep off nervous exhaustion, cry to relieve tension, talk out problems with friends, work off or play off depression, get out with friends, or see a doctor if the depression persists.

One of the biggest problems for the middle-aged, divorced person is meeting new people. Friends who are married either avoid inviting such "fifth wheels," or they try to play cupid. Singles bars or dances are often filled with people simply looking for a little adventure and variety. A man usually has more luck than a woman, since he is freer to ask for dates and younger women are available to him. Great patience and openness to new experience are required for those searching for new companionship.

It is true that much of the stigma attached to divorce is

vanishing. Also, new divorce laws, like the ones passed recently in California, make the procedure less painful than it used to be. No longer does blame have to be placed on one party in California divorce petitions; and no longer is the courtroom available as a battleground for airing grievances. Also, the waiting period has been reduced from one year to six months. Even the term "divorce" has been eliminated from California's record books; the procedure is now known as "dissolution of marriage."

Whether the easier divorce laws will enhance the temptation to end marriage as "just one of those things that didn't work out," or whether it will simply provide more opportunity for couples to end a deadlocked marriage and move to a more abundant and happier life is not known at this point. The divorce reform has brought new esteem to women, in particular. No longer is a woman bound to a marriage for her sense of worth and for her security. Changes in her conditions, toward greater economic independence, sexual freedom, and the physical means to stay looking and feeling younger, have no doubt increased the woman's tendency to turn to divorce in an unhappy marriage. On the other hand, the woman is learning that she has a right to happiness and personal fulfillment, too, and if her marriage does not provide that, then she has the ability to seek it either in a life alone or in another marriage.

What does continue to count is that a couple make an honest attempt to make their marriage work. Then if it does not, they must have the honesty and courage to admit the failure. If marriage as a religious covenant and/or a legal ceremony means anything at all, two people must enter wedlock intending to stay together and fight through all the struggle that takes. Such an understanding is hard to reconcile with a recent report that a British plan is afoot to provide "divorce insurance." That is, a means whereby a couple would start paying into a fund immediately upon marrying so that, if and when the marriage is dissolved, this fund would pay for the court action. The initiator of the plan defends it on the basis that since most women work in their homes as housewives they should be insured against the risks of their occupation!

Whenever wedlock becomes deadlock the specter of divorce arises as a way to end the misery of the marital existence. But while six-sevenths of the divorced remarry, they must first undergo the hard, painful process of finding oneself again in the status of being a single person and having to forge a new relationship.

> Even divorced persons dislike the institution. Their distaste comes from firsthand experience. They have lost old and valued friends. They have become prey to unwelcome attention, often from the mates of married friends. Their status has changed. They have known moments of unendurable loneliness. They seldom encourage others to follow them, save as a last resort.[11]

Though the divorce laws have become more relaxed, the natural impulse to resist that which tears something apart lingers on.

Once two people have found each other and shared a life together, every effort should be made to maintain a mutually gratifying marriage. If, however, marriage is experienced only as a dreary set of deadlocked relationships—as cellmates, checkmates, roommates, or stalemates—and you genuinely long for something more meaningful, then go on and imagine a resolution to the spouse gap crisis with the help of suggestions set forth in the last chapter.

[11] *Ibid.*, p. 136.

VII

RESOLUTION: TOWARD BRIDGING THE SPOUSE GAP

For those couples unwilling to settle for either deadlock or divorce, the marriage drama enters yet another and final stage, one alive with possibility and anticipation. Perhaps a resolution to the spouse gap problem is possible.

This is not to imply that there are pat answers to the problem, or simple solutions, or that imagining the bridge will build it. Closing the gap takes time and patience and understanding. If you have seen the film that shows the building of the Golden Gate Bridge, you will remember that after the bridge towers were in place a kind of weaving rig was set up between them. The workers started with small wires strung from one tower to the other and gradually spun the wires back and forth, back and forth, until a cable emerged, bigger around than a man. Over and over these huge lines were woven, until finally the road across was suspended from them and the two bodies of land were connected. The suggestions in this chapter are like small wires, which make it possible for you to weave connecting cables and build your way to each other.

The task is not easy and results will not be "perfect." Hannah Green has made an apt remark in her novel *I Never Promised You a Rose Garden*. This is the story of a young girl who, with the help of her psychiatrist, struggles to re-enter the real world and to escape the imaginary world and the kingdom she has made up which now holds her captive.

At one point, the girl, Deborah, throws a bitter remark at her doctor, whom she calls Furii or Fire-Touch: "What good is your reality, when justice fails and dishonesty is glossed over and the ones who keep faith suffer." The response comes back:

> "Look here," Furii said. "I never promised you a rose garden. I never promised you perfect justice . . . and I never promised you peace or happiness. My help is so that you can be free to fight for all of these things. The only reality I offer is challenge, and being well is being free to accept it or not at whatever level you are capable. And I never promise lies, and the rose-garden world of perfection is a lie . . . and a bore, too!" [1]

We do not intend to suggest that following a few guidelines will make a rose garden of your marriage and fill it with happiness and peace. We lay down a challenge for each person to go beyond past misery and injustice and failure, to cease blaming others for present troubles, and to assume responsibility for contributing to the marital situation.

The next step, of course, is to be sure both spouses want the marriage to work. If one member is not willing to try to make mutual changes and adjustments, then it is doubtful that there will be progress past the deadlock or divorce stages. For those couples who see that their marriage is in trouble, and who desperately want to make a go of it, there can be surprising changes. While changing basic character traits at a mature age is difficult, conscious adjustments and modification of attitudes and habits can be made.

Space scientists point out that a slight mid-course correction is essential for a successful flight, and that a little change in mid-course has vast consequences later on. Similarly, a mid-course correction involving mutual change for middles-

[1] Hannah Green, *I Never Promised You a Rose Garden* (New York: Signet Books, 1964), p. 106.

cent marriages will bear significant fruits later on. This mutuality implies two things: basic respect for each other and a belief in the value of the relationship, despite its defects. Perhaps nothing "new" can be introduced into a marriage at middle age, but there can be a rearrangement of what is there, the formation of a new gestalt or configuration of meaning, around which the marital relationship is renewed and rebuilt.

There is a sense in which the whole world is involved in the task of forming new gestalts at this time. We have mentioned the many technological and scientific changes at work on society. We should not be surprised that marriage feels the shock waves of radical social change. The real "DP" or displaced person is the one who stays put and is unable to respond to changes taking place all around him. Marriage does not exist in a vacuum but constantly absorbs the buffeting blows of social crises.

Social change is occurring at a faster clip than any of us could have imagined. Values and standards are being tried and found wanting. But perhaps the "tearing down" that is going on in our time will at last rid us of façades and phony barriers and free us to communicate more personally and directly. Marriage is, in a sense, a microcosm for such exploration and growth.

Let us then face with anticipation the task of changing. For wherever there is a passion to know what life means to us, a quest for understanding and awareness, and a hungering to experience human existence more intimately, there is the possibility of the more abundant life. The abundance will not be in goals attained but will come as we mutually strive for relatedness and as we celebrate the struggle itself, with its delights and its pains, its rewards and its defeats. When we finally learn that life is pilgrimage and process we can relax and rejoice, for then we are free to be. The contemporary poet Joseph Pintauro has provided us with the motto for our search: "Nowadays to be on your way is to be home." [2]

To be on our way toward bridging the spouse gap is to have made contact with the other person and to know his or her support and comfort and presence in the process of living and growing together.

Such a perspective requires us to take a risk, to be daring in letting go of old defenses and self-images and views of marriage roles. One analysis of a possible new style for contemporary man has been suggested by Sam Keen. Western culture, he points out, has tended to be dominated by the way of the Greek god Apollo, a way embodying ideals of order, discipline, balance, and reason, a way in which limits are defined and rigidly held to, and in which the environment is manipulated to man's advantage. Mr. Keen proposes that we are rebelling against such a god of "oughts" and limitations and security, and that the image for us to seek today is found in the way of the Greek god Dionysius. Dionysius was in fact a strange, wild kind of god, originating in Thrace, where he reigned over fertility and energy force in nature. His way is that of the dance, the rhythmic unity of life as flux and movement, the celebration of ecstasy and play. "Dionysian man is . . . a pilgrim, a gypsy, a dancer. His security lies in learning to be at home on the road. By contrast Apollonian man is a homesteader who stakes out a territory with defined limits and possibilities and finds his security in the defense of this territory." [3] Whether we can or should choose the Dionysian way over the Apollonian way as a marriage model, Mr. Keen's point remains well taken. We do need to balance our rational, manipulative, aggressive approach to life and love with a freer, more feeling-

[2] Joseph Pintauro and Sister Corita, *To Believe in God* (New York: Harper and Row, 1968) .

[3] Sam Keen, "Manifesto for a Dionysian Theology," *Transcendence*, edited by Herbert W. Richardson and Donald R. Cutler (Boston: Beacon Press, 1969) , p. 43.

centered, accepting approach. Marriage is less a product to be made than a dance to be performed as the rhythm of life pulses in us uniting male and female, light and dark, joy and sorrow, aloneness and togetherness, sickness and health, richness and poorness.

Let us then discuss some elements involved in an attempt to bridge the spouse gap: (1) the necessity of affirming the partner as a unique person, Person to Person; (2) some practical ways a couple can begin to rediscover each other anew in marriage, Re-creating a Life together; (3) kinds of opportunities that are available for helping a couple in their search, Resources for Renewal; and, finally, (4) what couples might look forward to in their later years, Beyond the Valley of the Spouse Gap. Try these on for size as you imagine it like it might be for your marriage.

PERSON TO PERSON

"For many—perhaps most—people, the primary source of joy is other people. But joy implies the possibility of misery; where there is ecstasy, so is there agony; if hell is other people, so is the divine." [4]

Take a moment and think about your spouse. Imagine him or her as a person separate from any relationship to you—not as your wife or husband, nor the mother or father of your children, but as an individual with a unique past, with special talents, and with a personal history. It is from such a vantage point that we must always relate to another, even after twenty years of marriage, for only when we acknowledge the personhood of each other can we truly relate. The gap widens between us and our spouses when we forget to see the other as a feeling, growing, changing person, when we take him or her for granted and expect certain roles and patterns to be fulfilled on our terms.

[4] Schutz, *Joy*, p. 117.

185

Now begin to feel the difference between expected marital images of behavior and a real, person-centered relationship in considering these factors: a *mother* never tires or gets sick, but the person you married can tire and does become sick. A *doctor's wife* (or minister's, or teacher's, or counselor's, or executive's!) is understanding and is never lonely, but the person you married does get impatient and lonely. A *wife* is responsive to her husband and so is always ready to respond to his sexual advances with loving tenderness, but the person you married has feelings that are sometimes expressed more appropriately in other ways. A *husband* is self-confident and assertive in his work, but the person you married has his self-confidence threatened and shaken at times. A *father* can be depended upon, and is happy, to be the primary breadwinner and protector of the family, but the person you married sometimes feels taken-for-granted and unnecessary, apart from bringing home the bacon. A *husband* is always a confident and attentive lover who takes initiative, but the man you married gets tense and anxious and needs affection and comfort.

Our point is that no one is married to an image or a role; everyone is married to a *person*—who is the same, yet not the same, today as yesterday. And the spouse gap can only be bridged when couples begin recognizing and affirming that reality. It is not too late to make this person-to-person discovery.

Of course relating to others (including the spouse) as persons necessitates regarding oneself as a person as well. We have already talked about the lack of ability to *feel*, which therapists report is a primary symptom of people seeking counseling help today. Along with that difficulty is the related inability to see the unique character of one's own experience. To finally accept the historical developments which made us what we are and from there to accept the flow of experience as our own is to be able to recognize the source from which we enter into freely chosen relationships and from which our personal growth develops. Rollo May speaks of this experiencing of feeling that "I-am-the-one-who-has-these-wishes," as a kind of manifesto for the impulse to relate across the spouse gap:

> This is the dimension of accepting one's self as having a world. If I experience the fact that my wishes are not simply blind pushes toward someone or something, that *I* am the one who stands in this world where touch, nourishment, sexual pleasure, and relatedness may be possible between me and other persons, I can begin to see how I may do something about these wishes.[5]

In this way one can trust himself to life, and be responsible for choosing a certain course, for relating in certain ways. Such is the basis by which we lay hold of our own personhood, respect that of the other, and find together a way of reconciliation.

Sometimes we are afraid to trust ourselves to life for fear we will be inadequate when the chips are down. Such despair is voiced by one of the characters in Edward Albee's remarkable play about middle-aged marriages, *A Delicate Balance*. The central couple, Tobias and Agnes, are distressed to learn that their daughter, Julia, is running away from her fourth husband. Agnes challenges Tobias to talk to his daughter, to try, at least once, to find the right tools of persuasion to send her back to a man she has married. Tobias, with great effort, finally agrees that perhaps he can find some words with which to achieve communication with her. But then he hesitates over the problem beyond the problem. What if he succeeds in breaking through the wall between them, what if they are able to struggle with agony to the place where they finally reached rapport, *then* what would he say?

Such barriers exist between friend and friend, parent and child, husband and wife. With silence or with meaningless sounds we bombard the wall between us, fearing that if we

[5] May, *Love and Will*, p. 266.

penetrate the wall we will have nothing of meaning or significance to say.

But now is the time to risk such a breach, to face each other as persons, with all that may mean. Unless we attempt such a confrontation we are lost anyway. Time passes, whether we fill it with events and experiences or not. "And," the wife in *A Delicate Balance* sighs, "after enough time, there's nothing left."

Once the wall of separation has been scaled, we can begin to relate by offering acceptance and forgiveness to each other. The most, perhaps, that any of us can give to another is our presence as a person, and that means recognizing our imperfections as well as both our need and capacity for forgiveness and acceptance. We can only really accept the other person when we experience in our own selves the meaning of the mutual separation. E. Mansell Pattison, a psychiatrist, suggests that failure to forgive others is, in the final analysis, the failure to forgive oneself. In forgiveness we extend our love to the one who has violated it. To face ourselves and each other honestly, and to accept and forgive can clear the decks for the new marital interaction as well as free the spouses to relate person to person. Indeed, as one author notes, "Today's conversation shows that people use the word 'forgiveness,' but by it they usually have in mind the sensation of freedom." [6]

Only that which is separate can really be related. Carl Jung, among numerous others, always emphasized the necessity for differentiation as a prerequisite to relationship. Things identical cannot be related, and their very sameness denies vitality or interest. When a husband and wife recognize themselves and each other as different persons, their love truly becomes a relational love, as opposed to the ideal of perfect union we discussed as characteristic of romantic love.

[6] James G. Emerson, Jr., *The Dynamics of Forgiveness* (Philadelphia: Westminster Press, 1964), p. 32.

188

Recognizing the need to relate person to person in marriage, we will find, does not make smooth sailing for the marriage. Relationships must always be worked at, and love will always be subject to certain tragic dimensions of life. The fact that each person is a free and autonomous individual means that there are clashes of will to be dealt with. The fact that each comes from a different background means that, even after twenty years of marriage, they will have misunderstandings and differences of opinion. Even a loving relationship can and sometimes does break down through failure or betrayal. And, of course, there always is the awareness that life is temporal—that love can fill our time, but it cannot stop the flow.

To recognize marital love as a relationship between two persons. Erich Fromm writes that "love is possible only if ous notion that love should be expressed by sacrifice of one's self for the other person. Such an impulse is noble, and we may indeed be called upon sometime to lay down our lives for others, but as a style for daily life in which to develop spouse relationships, it is disastrous.

The whole point of a mutually loving relationship rests in the necessity of two people's meeting each other as whole persons. Erich Fromm writes that "Love is possible only if two persons communicate with each other from the center of their existence, hence if each one of them experiences himself from the center of his existence." [7] Such love is a constantly growing, challenging experience for both parties, allowing neither one to idolize or sentimentalize the other or to project neurotic needs onto the other. But this love can come only if each partner is himself a centered self, aware of his own needs, feelings, and experiences.

Self-love, then, is not a thing to be denied and overcome. Far from it. Self-love is essential to our being able to love at all. Jesus' commandment to "love thy neighbor as thyself"

[7] Erich Fromm, *The Art of Loving* (New York: Harper Colophon Books, 1956), p. 103.

is testimony to the necessity for a person to respect his own feelings, capacities, and ideas. In this same vein the American psychiatrist Harry Stack Sullivan wrote that "when the satisfaction or the security of another person becomes as significant to one as is one's own satisfaction or security, then the state of love exists." [8] The key phrase to note is "as significant . . . as . . . one's own"—not more significant, but *as* significant. Unless such love of self is honored, there will come a time when feelings of resentment, hurt, betrayal, and unrequited love will find conscious or unconscious expression and will threaten the health of both the relationship and the personality structure of the individual. What is described here is not selfishness, which implies preoccupation with the self to the exclusion of others.

Just as we grow into ourselves and become true, centered identities, so also we grow, in a certain sense, into love. When we are young we erroneously try to throw ourselves into a love that will merge us with the other—an impossibility since neither self is really yet developed. What such early love can and should be, as suggested in a sentence by Rainer Maria Rilke, "is high inducement to the individual to ripen, to become world, to become world for himself for another's sake; it is a great and exacting claim upon him, something that chooses him out and calls him to vast things." [9] When the male and female come together not as opposites to complement each other, but as two human beings, there is a more human and more divine love which fulfills itself in responsible, free interaction: ". . . the love that consists in this, that two solitudes protect and border and salute each other." [10]

Such a view of relational love may lead us to rediscover

[8] Harry Stack Sullivan, *Conceptions of Modern Psychiatry* (New York: W. W. Norton and Co., 1953) , pp. 42-43.

[9] Rainer Maria Rilke, *Letters to a Young Poet* (New York: W. W. Norton and Co., 1934) , p. 54.

[10] *Ibid.,* p. 59.

also the meaning of love through sexual expression, whereby the act of intercourse is seen not as a duty to be done or a bestial appetite to be satisfied, but as a free giving and receiving of pleasure and affection. Sex and love are by no means synonymous, and many are the people who have mistaken sexual passion for love. But where one has genuine love of the other as person one has also the impulse toward intimacy of touch and feeling and toward the fulfillment of sexual desire.

> The fact that love is personal is shown in the love act itself. Man is the only creature who makes love face to face, who copulates looking at his partner. Yes, we can turn our heads or assume other positions for variety's sake, but these are variations on a theme—the theme of making love vis-a-vis each other. This opens the whole front of the person—the breasts, the chest, the stomach, all the parts which are most tender and most vulnerable—to the kindness or the cruelty of the partner. The man can thus see in the eyes of the woman the nuances of delight or awe, the tremulousness or the angst; it is the posture of the ultimate baring of one's self.[11]

We are discovering that sexuality enters and qualifies all aspects of a person's life and growth and human interaction. It is a creative source of energy and self-expression, as well as a language beyond words in which one self seeks to communicate with another self. Far too few of us entered marriage with adequate appreciation of our own sexuality, let alone the necessary preparation for understanding how to establish a sexual relationship with another person. Those taught to fear sex as sordid and dangerous, and conditioned never to let their feelings run away with them, can now perhaps feel free to relate totally to the person they love. As the most warmly shared and intimately responsive facet of relational love, the sex act becomes an occasion for two cen-

[11] May, *Love and Will*, p. 311.

tered selves to respond to each other in mutually fufilling needs that are not only biological, but psychic, emotional, and spiritual as well.

Present-day rebellion against traditional standards of sexual morality "is not always an irresponsible rejection of the faithfulness of monogamy, but an assertion of the positive power of sexuality to express, communicate, and release the self." [12] We have grown accustomed to the traditional assumption that sexual intercourse should be regarded primarily as a means for procreation, with marriage being the proper relationship for the rearing of children. And it is likely that this notion is now giving us a good deal of trouble. For the populaton explosion and the changing role of women call for a new view of sex and marriage. Hopefully the change will be in the direction of a belief more in keeping with the understanding of love as relationship, where sex takes its place as an act of communion in which love is expressed through the giving and receiving of two equal persons.

Where there is such a coming-together, person to person, there is a continuing reaffirmation of love as relationship and a supportive bridge across the spouse gap.

RE-CREATING A LIFE TOGETHER

Along with the necessity of seeing each other as unique persons, couples have the need to take conscious steps to close the gap that has developed between them. Let us then take a look at some of the specific ways this might be done. Remember that these ideas are not panaceas or cures, but suggestions that point to the process for finding new life together. Each couple must discover what works for them. Basic to our proposals, however, is the belief that the middlescent crisis in marriage need not lead to stagnant self-absorption and divisive deadlock, but can precipitate the outward search

[12] Daniel Day Williams, *The Spirit and the Forms of Love* (New York: Harper & Row, 1968), p. 232.

for renewal and re-creation. The resources of the human spirit to meet and triumph over difficulty are greater than we may imagine—if both partners want to find a resolution.

First, then, we suggest that you find a way to renew the meaning of your marriage together in terms of your present desires and expectations. Like so many other things in our day the very concept of marriage has become empty and eviscerated. The dynamic has been torn out of it. Certainly, too, the goals and ideals you originally had in mind when you embarked on your life together have been reached or have changed or are no longer appropriate to your situation. Now, at mid-life, is the time for spouses to discuss and to discover their mutual feelings about the meaning of their marriages.

Such renewal implies life in the present, the now—life sustained in person-to-person relationship by openness, communication, dialogue, and experimentation. The old reasons for marriage such as defense, economic survival, and procreation no longer apply to you. You must bring to light your own reasons and set your own future course.

Renewal of marriage also implies movement toward the future. Attempts to cling to the past and from that perspective to control and predict the marital relationship will crush the life from the marriage. If one longs for the past, he cannot enjoy or be fully present in the here and now, which is where we must do our living.

Part of living in the present is accepting the fact that everyone shows signs of aging at some time or another. It is foolish to hang on to youthful looks indefinitely. Certainly careful attention to proper clothes and colors, hair styles, and fashions can enhance appearance. Good posture, proper exercise, and diet are also important, both for looks and for general physical health. But knowing when to let go of the past and accept nature's will gracefully is the key to living one's present life. In the long run this moving with the process of life has distinct advantages.

It has been said that in youth a woman's good looks depend on her natural charms, but that after she passes forty it is her own fault if she is not beautiful, for after forty a woman's beauty depends much less than formerly on physical features and far more on her character and disposition. She is beautiful or ugly according to the kind of spirit that looks out of her eyes; she attracts or repels by the kindliness or bad temper which are expressed by the lines around her mouth. In other words it is her essential "being" that counts rather than the accidents of her physical make-up.[13]

Similar comments can be applied to men, of course. Emotional stability, self-confidence, mature understanding of human nature, good judgment, a healthy outlook on life, a sense of humor, sympathy, strength of character in coping with life's problems—these become infinitely more important than mere physical attractiveness or untempered energy, and they can only be realized through the experience of age.

As we have said, couples must find what works for them together. Perhaps your renewal of meaning in marriage will lead you to seek time apart for contemplation and reflection. There are couples who take part of their vacations each year for this. One spouse said that by the time he had been away from his wife a week he could hardly wait to get back to her! Maybe a sabbatical leave from marriage every ten years or so would bring partners back together with new perspective and vitality.

One concrete way to give expression to the renewal of marriage is to celebrate this new phase of married life in a remarriage ceremony. This may sound "far-out" to some middle-agers, but actually it makes good sense. Why not renew the vows which brought you together as man and wife in the first place, and this time know what they mean—for better or worse, for richer or poorer, in sickness and in

[13] Harding, *The Way of All Women*, pp. 284-85.

health? Those early days of setting-forth-to-play-house-to-gether are a thing of the past. Now you are free to establish a mature and responsible pledge of faithfulness.

One couple took advantage of their twenty-fifth wedding anniversary to have a remarriage ceremony. They used the same marriage service, including the same music, and the wife—with great delight!—wore the same wedding gown. This celebration was a deeply meaningful experience for them, their children, and their friends. At the very least, wedding anniversaries should become occasions for re-creating past memories of love and pleasure and good times.

Or perhaps you might want to do a new service for your remarriage ceremony, one in keeping with your new pledge as it reflects where you are now as a couple and as individual persons. Sharing the planning of such a service would be an exciting way to find out how each of you feels about your relationship—what you want to celebrate, what memories, events, growth, and learning you want to articulate.

Whether you use a traditional service or write your own comtemporary one, a remarriage ceremony in middlescence could launch your remaining life together with renewed meaning, joy, and vitality.

A second pointer for your exploration as you seek to bridge the spouse gap is to find common pursuits appropriate to your new age and stage. What had meaning at an earlier time may no longer be satisfactory in a relationship that has changed, and is changing. Over and over we return to the quote from Balzac: "Marriage must constantly conquer the monster that devours. Its name is habit." Finding common pursuits in study, in art and drama, in travel, and in other activities that will provide realms of meaning and conversational points of contact is essential.

Sharing activities may take some effort on the part of both spouses, especially when they involve going out. There are projects which can be carried on in the home, to be sure, but remember:

It is fun to go out once in a while and leave these walls—
not a large adventure, just a small one. Dinner and dancing
perhaps, or a show, or some interesting people to talk with
about interesting things. Later it may turn out that it would
have been more enjoyable to stay home, but at least one's
opinion would then be based on some evidence. But so often
when the man gets home from the day at the office, usually
after a commuting trip, he would like to take his shoes off
and stay there.[14]

So we encourage you to go places. Hike or camp or bicycle
or go to a movie together. But do something together often.
If you can't always agree on the activity, then take turns deciding what to do. You may find your interests are double
what they were. Psychologists tell us we tend to forget unpleasant things and to remember pleasing and shared experiences. Marriages become boring when there is no shared
experience. But each time you and your spouse have fun together you in effect make a deposit in a savings account.
There you are saving joys rather than dollars, with lots of
accumulated interest to draw on later.

Such common pursuits can be applied also to areas of
social service. Get involved in a political party, or church
activities, or social agency volunteer work and you may find
that as you give yourself to some form of service, your marital
health increases as well.

Ways should be found to include your spouse in the
pursuits you carry on alone. For instance, there is a corporation that sends brief, mimeographed minutes of its staff meetings home for wives to read. You men know how often you
come out of a staff meeting, maybe a church or a faculty or
a corporation pow-wow, and go home, and your wife asks,
"What happened?" You say, "Nothing much," because you
just don't feel like telling it, or because your mind draws a
blank. Literally you exclude the other person from your

[14] Rodenmayer, *I John Take Thee Mary*, p. 100.

world. So this corporation has experimented with sending minutes home so that particular types of intelligent questions can be raised by the wives. Such possible and appropriate sharing of the mind is an important part of the search for common pursuits, and makes home conversation much more interesting.

Each partner needs to be encouraged also to develop his own interests and potential; so part of the common pursuit may be encouraging the other in his individual development, whether in art, aesthetics, music, mechanics, sewing, reading, gardening, or so on. These personal areas of talent and skill become places where the spouse gap is bridged through mutual sharing.

A third way to help re-create your life together—and this may sound facetious!—is to keep alive the sense of chase. Hunters often say that the pursuit is more than half the fun, and may be more important than the kill or capture. When this sense of chase is terminated, either partner may drift or take the other for granted, or, more than likely, simply go to pot. To be sure, the sense of chase will not and should not be the romantic tumult it was in early youth, with bouquets of flowers (though such a surprise is nice sometimes!) , wild passion, and a literal chase around the car or couch. But a lively sense of pursuit in the manner of courtship attentiveness, persuasion, and spontaneity will keep the relationship exciting. Each spouse thereby affirms the partner continually as a desirable, needed person.

One minister/counselor tells of a couple, both moving toward their 60's, where the husband lay dying of cancer. One day as his wife entered the hospital room the husband said to the minister, "Look at that! Isn't she beautiful?" Such a small act is part of the chase we are talking about, a "calling forth" of the other, a way of articulating the fact that the spouse is cherished, appreciated, wanted, honored, and seen. Far from being taken for granted, this wife was still being courted.

While the sexual dimension is only part of the sense of the chase, it is an important part and provides the focal point for expressing feelings of intimacy and affection. One author, discussing sex in the middle years, writes: "It is important, not for the relief of the pent-up drives that characterize adolescence, but as a symbol of a union between two people who have learned to care deeply for each other. Its function in the mid-years is the affirmation of tenderness and the unspoken token of togetherness." [15] In such an understanding, then, the act of lovemaking grows out of the way of life and depends on the creation of a mood. Keeping alive the sense of chase for spouses means maintaining contact, by listening to the other, touching as you pass, speaking of how you feel, and respecting each other as persons. You don't own each other and can't expect instant response. Making love takes time to anticipate and experience the total act, and it takes imagination. Sexual intercourse actually begins when the two parties start to imagine and anticipate what is to come in their coming together. The first sensory changes begin to take place and the rhythm of the two persons begins to work together. Mixing the right ingredients for this chemical reaction is part of the art of lovemaking which couples who keep alive the sense of chase can cultivate over the years.

Also important, and we've touched on it before, is the willingness to be spontaneous about making love. Such spontaneity can recharge waning potency and bring spice back into the sex life—copulating at odd hours during the day, or first thing in the morning, or in a different place. This need not be a regular procedure, but it can be a pleasant and rewarding change. There are some people who cling to the old wives' tale that sex is debilitating to a middle-aged man. Actually, it can be just the tonic he needs to send him into the day's work with energy and exhilaration. The night may

[15] James A. Peterson, *Married Love in the Middle Years* (New York: Association Press, 1968) , p. 81.

not be the best time for intercourse, since physical tiredness and mental pressures may dampen the sexual mood.

Along this line, we should call your attention to an observation by Stanley Frank regarding commuters: "A man who lives in the suburbs may be more potent in an extramarital affair simply because the rendezvous is in town and he copulates before going through the drudgery of commuting." [16] For various reasons some middle-aged couples are examining whether their decision to remain in the suburbs is still valid. If the children are grown and gone, the house bigger than they need, their participation in outdoor activities curtailed, they might do well to return to the city where they would be closer to the husband's work. While it may be difficult at first for the wife to leave friends and comforts, she may gain a happier, more rested husband and eventually find advantages in the city intellectually stimulating.

In the long run, keeping alive the sense of chase can do what all the affairs cannot—it can allow for the kind of imagination and experimentation which a trusting relationship with one partner can make possible. For most people variety through different partners is less rewarding ultimately than a spontaneous satisfying relationship with the single other person. On this point Mr. Frank makes an apt remark:

The genuine test of ardor is sustaining it with one partner. A husband and wife who still arouse mutual excitement after three or four decades are more proficient in the arts of love than the noisome "celebrities" who infest gossip columns, bouncing from pillow to bedpost with a parade of boudoir athletes. They usually wind up sleeping with rejects like themselves.[17]

A fourth way to go at the task of bridging the spouse gap by re-creating a life together is to reserve time for each other

[16] Frank, *The Sexually Active Man Past Forty*, pp. 198-99.
[17] *Ibid.*, p. 179.

in your marriage. In a sense, this suggestion underlies the previous three points, for unless you take time for yourselves together you won't be able to see each other as persons, find common pursuits, or keep alive the sense of chase.

We have discussed previously how the kid-centeredness of our culture has allowed the children to create gaps in the husband-wife relationship. This gap must now be bridged over a period of time in which couples get to know each other again. If you still have children in the home in your middlescent years, begin now to reconsider your roles as parents and focus on your interaction as spouses. You were two people committed to a life together before you had children and you will be that after your children are grown and on their own. This doesn't minimize your responsibility for their growth and nurture, but it emphasizes your need to reserve time for the two of you as well.

Such time together can come through your engagement in common pursuits, as you take trips and go out together. Speaking to this need for spouses to have privacy and time alone, an author suggests that "even a weekend in a nearby motel can be days of wonder and joy." [18] Some couples have revived the custom of teatime or the cocktail hour together at the end of the day. A certain couple has set aside one afternoon a week to visit museums in the city, have dinner out, and then take in a show.

Another way to reestablish the sense of intimacy by taking time together is through sharing memories. Perhaps you will find new closeness by looking through photograph albums together, reading old letters, visiting places from your courtship and early marriage days, or straightening up the attic or the basement. Time and again such occasions for sharing leads one spouse to say, "Why I never knew you felt that way!" or "I didn't know you even knew that!" and memory serves as a springboard for self-disclosure which draws a couple together.

[18] McCready, *Our Bed Is Flourishing,* p. 46.

And, of course, the sexual relationship should allow for time together. One author beautifully describes what taking time for each other in this context can mean:

> Lovemaking in its intimacy prompts a couple to do what modern couples seldom have time to do: Talk. It provides quiet hours of conversation, of shared griefs and successes, the sadnesses of partings and the overflowing joy of return. It knits the emotions, feelings, and instincts of the couple together. It does not allow them to live together like college roommates or mere chums; it introduces them to a wholly different—and infinite—dimension of intimacy.[19]

Such shared companionship can bring light to the darkness of human despair and fear, and can make of the marriage a true uniting of two persons in relational love.

Finally, a fifth way to go about the task of re-creating a life together involves the process of self-renewal. Or to put it in the vernacular: "Learn, baby, learn." This means recognizing that much of our disinterest and boredom with each other stems from the simple fact that we are not terribly interesting people to each other. Too often we quit growing, quit learning, quit renewing ourselves. Middlescence is just the time to start changing all of that and to embark on the task of continuing education throughout the rest of our lives.

The contemporary Jewish theologian, Rabbi Abraham Heschel, has suggested that the question for us is not Hamlet's "to be or not to be," but rather the vital question "How to be and how not to be." Pursuit of such a question takes us into many paths of life exploration. To be aware of contemporary issues and historical forces is important, for instance. It is important also to seek fulfillment in community life beyond home, family, and personal pleasure. Certainly a sense of humor which helps us gain perspective on ourselves

---

[19] Novak, "Frequent, Even Daily Communion," p. 101.

and takes the edge off emotional tension is important. As technology makes more and more leisure time available to us we have the opportunity to cultivate all the marvelous arts of living and loving. We can learn, we can grow, we can become more aware and informed and interesting if we will but discipline ourselves to transform the middlescent malaise and take hold of the opportunities for self-renewal.

We tend to forget that cerebral functions are at their peak by the middle years. This presents us with the challenge to use those powers to their fullest. In middlescence the focus is a different one for the most part.

> There needs now to be a shift in the individual's life away from physical activity and toward mental activity, coupled with a determined and organized effort to maintain and increase mental flexibility. Only thus may he capitalize on the freedom to dispose and control his use of time, a freedom that is present for the first time in any significant degree since early childhood.[20]

Self-renewal will result in our being more interesting to ourselves *and* to our spouses. George Leonard, renowned writer in the area of education, has defined learning as ecstasy. Could we but lay hold of this ecstasy as we continue to learn and grow in our middle years we would become more vital, enriched, and joyous persons—and more interesting to be around.

Such continuing growth must be cultivated, because more often than not we tend to cling to the past in an attempt to identify with the vitality of our youth rather than risk moving on to more mature levels of learning. We are always capable of change, but as we resist changing we place ourselves in danger of solidifying early patterns into a rigid

[20] Thomas B. Robb, *The Bonus Years* (Valley Forge: The Judson Press, 1968), p. 90.

form. Now is the time to break through such an impasse. Why not?

Much of our continuing education in middlescence needs to be based on coming to know ourselves as persons rather than as instruments to accomplish certain tasks. At this period in life, when we are questioning values, evaluating goals, and puzzling the question of meaning, we are probably more receptive than we will ever be to discovering and becoming the self each of us truly is. Dr. Carl Rogers, writing of his work as a psychotherapist, describes one essential change which takes place as his patients get in touch with their feelings and experiences and begin to trust their own organisms.

> Clients seem to move toward more openly being a process, a fluidity, a changing. They are not disturbed to find that they are not the same from day to day, that they do not always hold the same feelings toward a given experience or person, that they are not always consistent. They are in flux, and seem more content to continue in this flowing current. The striving for conclusions and end states seems to diminish.[21]

As a man or woman learns how to continue becoming the person he or she is, it is increasingly possible to discover the self-integration and the satisfying social interaction each of us longs for so desperately. Man is more than a pleasure-seeking creature, and, once he faces the fact that life lived on the pleasure principle leads to satiety and boredom, he stands ready to enter those experiences which yield a fuller, richer, and more vital life. Middle age is not too late to cultivate the kind of elasticity of the personality which helps us learn and change. In the process we will discover that our self-renewal has made us more interesting to our spouses as well as ourselves.

[21] Carl R. Rogers, *On Becoming a Person* (Boston: Houghton Mifflin Co., 1961), p. 171.

RESOURCES FOR RENEWAL

It may not be enough simply to set out to re-create a life together in the ways described in the previous section. Perhaps it is too hard to break old patterns, or perhaps you can't get together as a couple to start the journey, or perhasp you just need more specific help on how to arrive at a one-to-one understanding in your relationship. Here let us look at some helps and aids outside the marriage, remembering that these suggestions are of value only where both spouses willingly try to improve their marriage.

First, of course, there is the availability of professional help. Sometimes one or the other spouse will benefit from individual therapy, but more and more counselors regard work with one half the couple as detrimental to the marriage. The person getting help grows in awareness and understanding while the other does not. Since marriage is an interacting system, it eventually breaks down if one part is operative and the other is not. Some counselors deal with the family as a unit where children are still present in the household. There also are counselors who work as co-therapists, a man and a woman together, relating to the husband and wife with a double measure of perspective and insight.

Oddly enough, people are hesitant about seeking outside help unless they are in big trouble, and even then they may find it difficult. We do not hesitate to hire a dentist for our teeth or a mechanic for our car, but there is widespread reluctance to admit we need marital help. If we could really accept the fact that continuous and perfect harmony in marriage is impossible since marriage is a changing process involving two individual persons, then maybe we could see that such help from time to time is a mature, responsible approach to maintaining a creative relationship.

Also available are various group-counseling opportunities, where several married couples meet with a therapist for weekly group psychotherapy sessions. This procedure has been helpful as a way to get past the belief that the problems a particular couple faces are somehow unique and shameful. Realization that others have difficulties too (sometimes of the same kind) can do much to provide a supportive atmosphere in which spouses can work through their difficulties. Time and again we discover that what seem to us to be the most personal and private feelings or experiences actually are quite general. A group atmosphere tends to facilitate communication between spouses as they are encouraged by the other members to engage in honest exchange, and as they discover that their free expression of opinion does not drive the spouse away. The couples also provide feedback to each other as they observe nonverbal behavior and unconscious patterns of interaction. The presence of co-therapists in this process is helpful in providing role models which the couples can identify with or emulate.

If intensive, ongoing therapy is not possible or desirable, spouses may find opportunities for work with other couples and professional counselors on weekend retreats. Such activities are often sponsored by churches as "spiritual retreats" in which couples can have a quiet time together for reevaluation and inspiration. One couple has gone on this kind of retreat each year for the last three years and feels it is a primary source of renewal for their marriage. Over the weekend, couples have a chance for discussion with professional counselors as well as free time for doing things together.

The majority of marriages could be made workable, perhaps, if spouses would seek a yearly marital checkup with a competent professional "marriage doctor." Such a checkup would keep the partners aware of where their relationship is changing, how each is growing, and what their trouble spots are, as well as save them from taking each other for granted and letting them consciously appreciate the good things about their marriage. Recognizing that such an annual checkup is not likely to happen on a widespread scale, authors William Lederer and Don Jackson have devised a procedure whereby couples can conduct a "do-it-yourself" checkup. The full plan is described in their book *The Mirages of Marriage,* and we heartily recommend it to you for your use.

The authors provide four different methods whereby couples can utilize the plan and check up on their marriage. In Method A the spouses isolate themselves and each makes the marital appraisal alone. For obvious reasons this is considered the least effective use of the material. In Method B the two sit together and perform a joint evaluation of their marital state; and in Method C the two meet in the presence of a third individual who listens to them and reflects back what he hears. In Method D two couples meet together in an effort to share the function of judging and appraising each other's marital interactions. As a basis for the appraisal the authors provide some forty-five questions about the marriage itself and an Interpersonal Comparison Test, which brings to light differences in backgrounds, opinions, and values.

One of the most interesting parts of this do-it-yourself resource for bridging the spouse gap is a series of exercises Lederer and Jackson have devised to assist couples in changing old patterns of relating and to encourage exploration in areas previously avoided. They outline five sessions for the spouses to work through, followed by regular full-scale discussion meetings. These sessions are designed to help couples establish a workable, constructive *quid pro quo,* or "something for something" arrangement for their interaction. Recognizing that bargaining in marriage is essential, the next step is then to decide what kind of bargaining a certain couple has to do, and how they should do it. The point is not to try to solve the marital strife "by making sacrifices," or "giving in," or even by "being more loving." These solutions are unilateral and have little constructive effect because they do not come to terms with the basic difficulties. A couple must do it together, in a give-and-take atmosphere of mutual respect and understanding. By becoming aware of each other's debating tricks and behavior when trying to get one's way, couples have a much better chance of gaining "equal time" in their marriage game and thereby finding it more mutually satisfying.

Esalen Institute has helped many couples get in touch with themselves. To cite one of many exercises as an example for bridging the spouse gap: The couple are seated facing each other. First one spouse, then the other is to complete this sentence: "Our marriage would be a lot better if—" After finishing the sentence, each person is to repeat back what he or she heard the other one saying. Then each person is to apply his own remark to himself to test the extent of projection involved in the comment. Thus one wife stated, "Our marriage would be a lot better if you quit going to so damn many meetings." Applying this remark to herself, it suddenly dawned on her that she was the one, or at least she was also, going to too many meetings.

There are many other kinds of questionnaires, workshops, basic encounter groups, checklists, and counseling resources available. You will have to seek them out—they won't just come to you. Your own willingness to seek outside resources and your openness to such new experiences are the primary requirements for bringing into your marital relationship the kind of renewal whereby you can bridge the spouse gap and find new life together.

BEYOND THE VALLEY OF THE SPOUSE GAP

Hopefully the suggestions in this chapter have prodded you to imagine your marriage like it might be. Continue that imagining for a moment. You have faced the gap and the attendant problems of middlescence; you have sought help and worked through ways to rediscover your spouse. You have found ways to re-create a life together. Now what?

Well, studies show that if couples can weather the storm of their middle years, if they can pass through the valley of the spouse gap, having faced all the fears and dangers that lurk there, then the outlook is very bright. As men and women move into their fifties having adjusted to their crises they have a higher rate of marital happiness and satisfaction. Often there is a kind of Indian summer or a second honeymoon in store for them.

People do seem to sense that this is true. Not long ago the Question Man in the *San Francisco Chronicle* asked seven people, "Do couples enjoy themselves more before or after 40?" Without exception they all said "after." To support their answers they cited such things as the fact that they could turn their attention to things other than working, raising children, and getting used to each other. If we can only recognize it, the middle years are of tremendous value as they bring us richness of experience, a tempering of impetuosity, and knowledge of ourselves and others. If we can begin now to cultivate those arts of living, we will reach the other side of the valley of the spouse gap with insight and genuine maturity.

Thus one doctor observes, "In good marriages when romantic love has sung its brief song, a soberer and wiser couple remain, disillusioned and perhaps a bit grim, but not defeated." [22] Such spouses know that marriage must be worked at, that by utilizing their resources they can make their partnership work, that by living life as pilgrimage and process their love will be part of their becoming.

> Sex will not be the thrilling adventure it once was, but it will still be gratifying. They will be satisfied with this and not seek new partners with whom to attempt to rediscover the old thrill, and its inevitable chill. Such a marriage, in spite of the loss of romance,—indeed, because of it,—can become constantly better and more rewarding. Children may be born and grow up and leave, and the husband and

[22] Philip Solomon, "Love: A Clinical Definition," *The New England Journal of Medicine*, March 3, 1955, 350.

wife still share all this too as their lives intertwine and intermingle.[23]

While passion may plateau out with the years, and with it the previous sense of complete and utter devotion to the partner, a mutual feeling of honesty, tolerance, respect, and a desire to remain together can make the marriage one of satisfaction and fulfillment.

As the struggle for identity becomes resolved with the passing through middle age, the sexual relationship often becomes more stable, realistic, and comfortable. Generally speaking, men usually stop making passes at other women after middlescence, realizing that intercourse with the wives they know is better than the hassle of creating opportunities for sex with many others. As one man said to his wife as he continued to look at pretty young girls even though he had no intention of straying: "When I stop looking, you can throw me out, because I'll be dead. If you think I could chase her and start all over again, you're crazy. Why should I spend twenty years helping her to grow to what you are now?" [24] When a couple survives together to their later years, having continued to respect and cherish each other, they may discover the kind of fulfillment that springs from shared love.

In this light, perhaps, it becomes clear what may be the ultimate purpose and meaning of married life, the promise that, after the glamour of youth has faded and the struggle of the middle years is over, two people will be together in close intimacy as they enter the final phase of their lives. A man recently remarked on this, saying that he and his wife had suddenly found each other again, and that part of their discovery came as they projected forward into the later years of their lives and realized they would want to be together then. The early death of one or the other partner may cut short

[23] *Ibid.*
[24] McCready, *Our Bed Is Flourishing*, p. 93.

this future reality, but the relationship which embodies such a desire cannot but make a difference in the lives of the two persons no matter how much time they actually have together.

It may well be a consciousness of our mortality that makes love and companionship so rich and deep a feeling. Abraham Maslow suggests this as he described his experience in recuperating from a heart attack:

> The confrontation with death—and the reprieve from it— makes everything look so precious, so sacred, so beautiful that I feel more strongly than ever the impulse to love it, to embrace it, and to let myself be overwhelmed by it. My river has never looked so beautiful. . . . Death, and its ever present possibility makes love, passionate love, more possible. I wonder if we could love passionately, if ecstasy would be possible at all, if we knew we'd never die.[25]

Scientists are telling us that, in the not-too-distant future, life may be prolonged for hundreds of years. Ways are now being discovered to affect cell structure and to reduce aging, as well as to replace organs and body parts that wear out. Even now the population over 75 in the United States is increasing at a rate two and a half times that of the general population. Imagine, if you can, living through parts of two centuries! No one can say now whether such advances will be assets or liabilities, and certainly a whole new set of problems will arise: problems related to work and retirement; to life and health insurance; to social relations among generations; to aging control *versus* birth control; to whether it is possible for two people to stay together in marriage for 150 years!

For us, of course, this prolonged life is not yet an option, and many may sigh with relief. But the point is, we must rapidly find ways of handling the aging process so that the evening years are not wasted in bitterness, isolation, insecu-

[25] Quoted in May, *Love and Will*, p. 99.

rity, and frustration. Too many of our old people have nothing to do and nothing to do it with. As a society we must encourage the development of resources so that a person can enter old age with a wide repertoire of interests to pursue. We have held on too long to the ethic that lauds work as the chief end of man and as the indication of his worth. Now, in middle age, we must start to prepare ourselves for a new phase in our lives.

Dr. E. Mansell Pattison has identified three general cultural attitudes toward dying as: death-defying, death-denying, and death-accepting. Western civilization, he points out, has traditionally been characterized by the first, but in modern times has shifted to the second—hence our preoccupation with youth, romance, and pleasure. Here death is feared and held off as an intrusion into what we imagine should be eternal existence. Pattison goes on to note that death finally comes to all (whether at 80 years or 175 years, we might add!). "The importance of an appropriate death is that dying is not an extraneous foreign process but rather it is a process integrated into the style, meaning and sequence of that which has gone before. The concrete nature of each man's appropriate death will be different, but can be appropriate for him." [26]

It seems right that we should have within the flow of life a period in which to gather in and enjoy the fruits of our labors. Our culture does not let us regard our later years in this way, however. Primitive people seem to have had a simple, naïve instinct about accepting old age as part of the natural course of life, turning duties over to the younger people so that they might retire from the scene. Our sophisticated, more ego-conscious state of civilization has made us fearfully and poignantly aware of impending separation from life as a kind of inescapable defeat. Now we need to work our way to a higher level of consciousness in which the last

[26] E. Mansell Pattison, M.D., "The Experience of Dying," *American Journal of Psychotherapy*, January, 1967, p. 41.

stage of life can be welcomed as well as the others. While we cannot return to the primitive simplicity of accepting the life process without question, perhaps we can push through the complexity of modern thought and feelings to a new simplicity. We may find that reviving the practice of spiritual retreats in later life might provide a context within which we could meet and wrestle with the ultimate concerns of life and meaning, an endeavor for which we had little time in the earlier stages.

Those of us who have been present with some person who has borne suffering and death with dignity and integrity will recognize the validity of this higher level of death-accepting consciousness. Carl Jung, who lived to be eighty-five himself, pressed for continuing inward development throughout all one's life, which meant granting meaning to the afternoon and evening of life as well as to the morning. Carrying on Jung's vision, Esther Harding also calls attention to the way the human organism rallies to new heights even as life crumbles:

> When in later life the attention withdraws from the external world it may be that the life-energy gathers itself together for its last and most significant creative act. The human being *himself* becomes the recipient of his own life-energy. He is liberated from identification with the outer world. He is free, as Whitman sings, "with the delicious near-by freedom of death" and like a free man can devote himself to the final task of his life which is—to use Jung's phrase—the *achievement* of death.[27]

Some may find this last discussion somewhat morbid, perhaps. Certainly it is not our intention to depress our readers by premature consideration of end-things in life. But it *is* our hope to point to areas of life for which we must prepare, and to possibilities that will enhance our capacity for living

[27] Harding, *The Way of All Women*, pp. 292-93.

deeply and creatively. This is part of what lies beyond the valley of the spouse gap—the opportunity to pursue yet a new stage of life in the company of a partner you know and love in ever new and changing ways. He or she is working through an internal process as well as you are. To be able to come to grips with the middlescent crisis and to emerge with some growing degree of honesty, mutual respect, and appreciation, some increased sense of freedom and imagination concerning personal interaction is to have found a pearl of great price which can add luster to your remaining years.

The well-made marriage does not just happen automatically, nor is it a stroke of luck or a miracle; it is the sum of all the elements we have discussed here. It is a quest in which remembering it like it was, facing it like it is, and imagining it like it might be come together into a unity of expression which reflects the ongoing process of discovery characteristic of all life and love. It is an achievement, a constant movement of a couple through purpose, passion, or suffering to new perception. It is a drama in every sense of the word— situation, conflict, complication, suspense, crisis, climax, and resolution—in which the script is written as the play unfolds and for which there is no end.

The well-made marriage is a rhythm in which gaps are inevitable, but in which also spouses can build bridges to close the gaps if both are willing to risk knowing and being known. It is a basic paradigm for human relationships, as male and female enter into a responsible, responsive, relational rapport in which both grow and change and interact together and with others, and so fulfill their destinies as living and loving creatures.

BIBLIOGRAPHY

Bach, George R., and Wyden, Peter. *The Intimate Enemy.* New York: William Morrow and Co., 1969.

Bayer, Ann. "Beginning Again in the Middle," *Life,* June 12, 1970.

Bergler, Edmund, M.D. *The Revolt of the Middle-Aged Man.* New York: The Universal Library (Grosset & Dunlap), 1954.

Blood, Robert O., Jr. *Marriage.* New York: The Free Press, 1962. A revised edition of *Anticipating Your Marriage,* 1955.

Callahan, Sidney Cornelia. *Exiled to Eden: The Christian Experience of Sex.* New York: Sheed & Ward Search Book, 1969. Originally published under the title *Beyond Birth Control* in 1968.

————. "Human Sexuality in a Time of Change," *The Christian Century,* August 28, 1968.

Clinebell, Howard J., Jr., and Clinebell, Charlotte H. *The Intimate Marriage.* New York: Harper & Row, 1970.

de Rougemont, Denis. *Love in the Western World.* Translated by Montgomery Belgion. Revised and augmented edition. Originally published in France in 1939 as *L'Amour et l'Occident.* New York: Doubleday Anchor Book, 1956.

Driver, Tom F. "On Taking Sex Seriously," *Christianity and Crisis,* October 14, 1963.

Earnshaw, George L. *Serving Each Other in Love.* Valley Forge, Pa.: Judson Press, 1967.

Emerson, James G., Jr. *The Dynamics of Forgiveness.* Philadelphia: Westminster Press, 1964.

Fairchild, Roy W. "Parental Stress in Protestant Homes: Clues from Research," *Sex, Family and Society in Theological Focus.* Edited by J. C. Wynn. New York: Association Press, 1966.

Frank, Stanley. *The Sexually Active Man Past Forty.* New York: The Macmillan Co., 1968.

Fromm, Erich. *The Art of Loving: An Enquiry into the Nature of Love.* New York: Harper Colophon Books, 1956.

Gartner, Mike. "The Silent Generation Meets the Class of 1970," *Saturday Review,* August 15, 1970.

Green, Hannah. *I Never Promised You a Rose Garden.* New York: New American Library Signet Book, 1964.

215

"Growing Old in America," *Time*, August 3, 1970.

Harding, M. Esther. *The Way of All Women*. New York: Longmans, Green and Co., 1933.

Hunt, Morton. *The Affair: A Portrait of Extra-Marital Love in Contemporary America*. New York: New American Library (World), 1969.

Keen, Sam. "Manifesto for a Dionysian Theology," *Transcendence*. Edited by Herbert W. Richardson and Donald R. Cutler. Boston: Beacon Press, 1969, pp. 31-52.

Kronhausen, Eberhard, and Kronhausen, Phyllis. *The Sexually Responsive Woman*. New York: Ballantine Books, 1965.

Lederer, William J., and Jackson, Don D., M.D. *The Mirages of Marriage*. New York: W. W. Norton and Co., 1968.

Lee, Robert. *Religion and Leisure in America*. Nashville: Abingdon Press, 1964.

Levinson, Harry. "On Being a Middle-Aged Manager," *Harvard Business Review*, July-August 1969.

Levy, John, and Munroe, Ruth. *The Happy Family*. New York: Alfred A. Knopf, 1938.

Mace, David R. *Success in Marriage*. Nashville: Abingdon Press, 1958.

May, Rollo. *Love and Will*. New York: W. W. Norton and Co., 1969.

Mayer, Thomas. "Middle Age and Occupational Processes: An Empirical Essay," *Sociological Symposium*, No. 3, Fall 1969.

McCready, Robert B., M.D. *Our Bed Is Flourishing: A Gynecologist Looks at Sex, Love and Marriage*. New York: Sheed & Ward, 1969.

McLaren, Robert B., and McLaren, Homer D. *All to the Good: A Guide to Christian Ethics*. New York: World Publishing Co., 1969.

Novak, Michael. "Frequent, Even Daily Communion," *The Catholic Case for Contraception*. Edited by Daniel Callahan. London: Macmillan & Co., 1969.

Oden, Thomas C. *The Structure of Awareness*. Nashville: Abingdon Press, 1969.

Pattison, E. Mansell, M.D. "The Experience of Dying," *American Journal of Psychotherapy*, Vol. XXI, January 1967.

Peterson, James A. *Married Love in the Middle Years*. New York: Association Press, 1968.

Pintauro, Joseph and Sister Corita. *To Believe in God*. New York: Harper & Row, 1968.

"The Pleasures and Perils of Middle Age," *Time*, July 29, 1966.

Reuben, David R., M.D. *Everything You Always Wanted to Know About Sex*—*But Were Afraid to Ask*. New York: David McKay, 1969.

Rilke, Rainer Maria. *Letters to a Young Poet*. Translated by M.D. Herter Norton. Rev. ed. New York: W. W. Norton and Co. (1934), 1954.

"The Rising Pressures to Perform," *Time*, July 18, 1934.

Robb, Thomas Bradley. *The Bonus Years: Foundations for Ministry with Older Persons.* Valley Forge, Pa.: Judson Press, 1968.

Rodenmayer, Robert N. *I John Take Thee Mary: A Book of Christian Marriage.* New York: Seabury Press, 1962.

Rogers, Carl R. *On Becoming a Person.* Boston: Houghton Mifflin (1961), 1970.

Rubenstein, Richard E. *Morality and Eros.* New York: McGraw-Hill Book Co., 1970.

Saul, Leon J., M.D. *Fidelity and Infidelity.* New York: J. B. Lippincott, 1967.

Schutz, William C. *Joy: Expanding Human Awareness.* New York: Grove Press, 1967.

Solomon, Phillip, M.D. "Love: A Clinical Definition," *The New England Journal of Medicine,* Vol. 252, March 3, 1955.

Sullivan, Harry Stack. *Conceptions of Modern Psychiatry.* New York: W. W. Norton and Co., 1953.

Updike, John. *Couples.* New York: Fawcett Crest Books, 1968.

Viorst, Judith. *Its Hard to Be Hip over Thirty . . . & Other Tragedies of Married Life.* New York: New American Library Signet Book, 1970.

Williams, Daniel Day. *The Spirit and the Forms of Love.* New York: Harper & Row, 1968.

Wrage, Karl. *Man and Woman: The Basics of Sex and Marriage.* Edited by Cooperrider, translated by Stanley S. B. Gilder. Philadelphia: Fortress Press, 1969.

INDEX